INCOMPLETE NRI

DEBASHIS JHA

Clever Fox® PUBLISHING
Chennai • Bangalore

CLEVER FOX PUBLISHING
Chennai, India

Published by CLEVER FOX PUBLISHING 2026

ISBN: 978-93-7500-354-0

FOREWORD

"Incomplete NRI" is a profound exploration of what happened to the soul when it is stretched across continents. It is always a state of incompleteness – carrying a piece of home that doesn't quite fit abroad and returning to a home that has continued to evolve without you.

The journey of a thousand miles often begins with a single step, but for the millions who leave their homeland in search of a new life, that journey never truly ends. It is a path marked by a constant negotiation between two worlds: the one we left behind and the one we are trying to build.

In Incomplete NRI, we are invited into the heart of this experience.

Writing this foreword is a particular honor for me because the author, Debashis, is more than just a talented writer; he is a dear childhood friend. Having known him since our earliest days, it has been a privilege to watch his journey unfold. Seeing him develop himself—not just professionally, but as a deep thinker and a voice for his community—has been truly inspiring. This book is a testament to that growth and to the maturity with which he now views the world.

Through these pages, he captures the quiet moments of longing, the sharp stings of cultural dissonance, and the resilient hope that defines the immigrant spirit. It is a narrative that speaks to anyone who has ever felt like an outsider, and a tribute to the courage it takes to define oneself on one's own terms.

Whether you are part of the diaspora yourself or simply a traveller on your own journey of self-discovery, Incomplete NRI offers a mirror to the universal search for belonging. It reminds us that while our origins may be fixed, our identities are ever-unfolding stories.

I am proud of my friend for bringing this important work to life. May it inspire you to embrace your own “incompleteness” and find the beauty in the spaces between.

– Dr Adity Bhushan;

Sr Director, Author, Educationalist

FOREWORD

India is a masterclass in beautiful chaos, and I can think of no better guide through its vibrant madness than DJ. With a wit as sharp as a street-side samosa and a remarkably observant eye, DJ captures those small, hilarious details that most travelers would blink and miss. This log isn't just a record of miles traveled, but a collection of the absurd and wonderful mishaps that seem to follow him everywhere. It is a joy to introduce this journey, which proves that navigating the subcontinent requires both a great sense of humor and 'Jugaads'. Buckle up for a front-row seat to the comedy of errors that only happens when DJ hits the road.

Brijesh Tripathi |
Friend and Philosopher | IIT Kanpur |
MBA, McCombs School of Business, UT Austin

FOREWORD

When Debashis first told me he was going to write about his recent trip to India, I smiled politely and assumed it would be a simple travel log—places, people and perhaps a few stories. What I did not expect was to find myself laughing out loud, nodding in recognition and, at the same time, feeling a quiet lump in my throat as I turned the pages.

Incomplete NRI is not just about miles traveled or cities visited. It is about that corner of the heart we carry with us wherever we go. Through his eyes, India becomes more than a destination; it becomes a living character, rooted deeply inside him and inside all of us. In these pages, we meet the traveler as he truly is- sometimes confused, often amused, always observant, and endlessly curious about the people and places he encounters. As you read, you will walk beside him through crowded streets and quiet thoughts, through laughter and longing.

As someone who knows him beyond these pages, I traveled alongside him too, feeling the emotion that belonging is rarely complete. Yet it is this very sense of incompleteness that makes us whole, bridging cultures, places, and, of course, differences. The simplicity he carries in his life is beautifully mirrored in his writing, and I am incredibly proud of this traveler.

What I love most about this book is its honesty. It does not pretend that travel is always glamorous. Instead, it embraces missed connections, cultural misunderstandings, the unexpected kindness of strangers, and the joy found in small, ordinary moments. His humor is gentle and self-aware, allowing readers to feel as though they are walking right beside him, sharing both the mishaps and the magic.

I am certain that, just as I have, you will find joy in this journey. It is in our incompleteness that we discover who we truly are.

Rupa
Dear Spouse

PREFACE

Incomplete NRI is my attempt to narrate the quiet triumphs and everyday poetry of a life lived across continents—where government offices can feel like battlegrounds, balconies turn into confession booths and a humble Dhaba meal can taste exactly like home.

This book captures my last trip to India in Jul-Aug 2025—a journey that began as a neat two-week plan and like most things in life, quietly stretched into almost a month. In that time, I moved through three bustling metropolises—Chennai, Delhi and Bangalore—along with Ranchi, my birthplace and the city that shaped me; Bokaro Steel City, my in-laws' home; and even a small village tucked away in the green heart of Jharkhand. Each stop had its own rhythm, its own flavor, and its own way of reminding me that India never travels light—it arrives with stories.

On paper, the mission was clear. Get my USA Work VISA stamped before the drop box program ends, Sell a nearly 20-year-old apartment heavy with memories. Upgrade to a new 3-BHK that reflected changing aspirations. Reactivate a long-dormant PAN card. Apply for an Aadhaar I never thought I'd need. Navigate registry offices, banking formalities and the fine art of standing in the right queue at the right time. Add Bangalore traffic, Delhi paperwork and visa deadlines ticking louder than common sense, and the plot swings comfortably between comedy and crisis.

But beyond the checklists and deadlines were the moments that truly mattered—playing cricket with my nephews in Bokaro, sipping tea in Ranchi's drizzle, driving through Jharkhand's emerald ghats where waterfalls seem to whisper secrets to the hills. These were the pauses between tasks, the unscheduled scenes that quietly reminded me that home isn't just a place on a map—it's a feeling that follows you around.

At its heart, this is not a travel guide or a procedural manual, though you'll find plenty of airports, paperwork, and overpriced coffee along the way. It's a story about movement—across cities and continents, yes, but also inward. About being an NRI who looks settled on the outside yet feels unfinished on paper and occasionally within.

I've tried to keep the style of this book natural, real, conversational, and above all—honest. No filters, no pretenses. Just the raw rhythm of life as it unfolded, with all its detours, small victories, and laugh-at-yourself moments. If these pages make you smile, remember your own journeys, or suddenly crave a plate of daal tadka, then the trip was worth it.

Because this isn't just my story.

It's the story of anyone who has lived between two worlds—carrying pieces of both and learning that being incomplete is sometimes what keeps us moving.

– Debashis Jha

CONTENTS

CHAPTER 1

ME AND MY FAMILY

I came to the USA for what I call my "second inning" in August 2012, along with my wife, Rupa, and our three-year-old daughter, Aarna.

The first inning was way back in 2007. I was in my 2nd year of marriage, and we spent about 18 months here. Honestly, that phase felt like an extended paid honeymoon—life was simple, responsibilities were light, and everything seemed new and exciting. Back then, my goal was clear: save some dollars, pay off a few liabilities in India, and return to my motherland.

We were in the heart of Silicon Valley, surrounded by tech giants like Yahoo, Sun Microsystems, Google and Apple. It felt surreal to live in a place that was shaping the future of technology while I was still figuring out my own future.

But this book isn't about that first inning. It's about the second one—the one that truly shaped me.

Now, you might be wondering why I chose the title **"Incomplete NRI."** That thought is what provoked me to write this book. It feels like the most fitting title for the stage of life I'm in—a stage where one foot is firmly in the USA and the other in India. I'm stretched across these two worlds—emotionally, mentally, and financially. And in many ways, that makes me feel incomplete.

The title became even more relevant after my last trip to India . As you read through the chapters, you'll slowly understand why this resonates so deeply with me.

CHAPTER 2

THE PLAN THAT WASN'T A PLAN

I had been thinking about going to India for a while, but honestly, there was no concrete plan. It was one of those discussions that kept floating around between me and Rupa—*When should I go? What all need to be done? How do I fit everything in?*

Then came the twist. A sudden announcement about the U.S. visa drop box policy changed everything. The new guideline said the drop box facility would no longer exist after September first week. However, those who had already booked an appointment before the first week of September could still avail it.

And guess what? I had already managed to grab a slot for 31st July. That is the only thing taken care of till now. That slot felt like a gold mine—like winning a lottery. But now the real challenge was to plan the entire trip around that milestone.

This wasn't just about using the drop box opportunity for one last time to get my U.S. visa stamped. There was a long list of tasks waiting for me in India.

First, I needed to get all the documents in order and sell my flat in Indirapuram, Ghaziabad—a property almost 20 years old and, let's just say, not exactly pampered by the tenants (sarcasm intended). Once that was done, the plan was to reinvest the money into a new property somewhere in the same area. Then came the task of finding a full-time helper for my in-laws in Bokaro, something we had been trying to figure out for quite some time. I took this as a personal challenge—and, honestly, a way to impress my wife. They say it right: a happy wife leads to a happy life. Of course, no trip to India feels complete without visiting my parents in my hometown, so that was on the list too. And finally, I had to sort out the banking mess—convert accounts into NRE and NRO and make sure everything was in line.

So, what started as a vague idea suddenly turned into a race against time. That visa slot became the anchor point for everything. The clock was ticking, and I had to make it all happen.

CHAPTER 3

LANDED IN INDIA

With all these plans and baggage—both literal and emotional—I booked my flight and landed in Chennai, India, on 30th July 2025. My drop box appointment was scheduled at Chennai VAC, so Chennai had to be my port of entry. My return ticket to the USA was for 16th August from New Delhi. I had made some tentative plans to wrap up everything and catch that flight back in time.

Only one miscalculation, I realized 16th August is my birthday. So, instead of celebrating with family or friends, I'd be spending it at an airport. *Let's see how that goes,* I thought.

I was an **Incomplete NRI** who had just landed in India. Why incomplete? Because everything about my identity felt scattered. My PAN was inoperable since I hadn't been filing income tax regularly in India. The main reason? It lacked the KYC check—it wasn't linked to Aadhaar. I had no Aadhaar card. Never took it seriously. A classic catch-22 situation.

My voter ID looked like it belonged to the Stone Age—completely useless. I had no active debit or credit cards in India.

To make matters worse, my ICICI bank account was locked, and my Bank of Baroda account was inactive, though it still had some money sitting there.

Standing there in Chennai, I felt incomplete—not just on paper, but inside.

The excitement of being back in India was real—the familiar smell of humid air, the chaos of the airport, the sound of people speaking in different languages. But underneath that excitement was a layer of anxiety. *Will I be able to finish everything in time? What if something goes wrong with the visa stamping? What if the property sale gets stuck?*

It was a strange mix of emotions—thrilled to be home yet burdened by the weight of unfinished tasks. I kept reminding myself: this trip wasn't just a vacation. It was a mission. And the clock had already started ticking.

CHAPTER 4

THE PEOPLE WHO MADE IT POSSIBLE

Every journey had its heroes, and mine was no different. If I was chasing completeness, these were the people who stood by me and made it happen.

First, there was **Arvind Ji**, the Chartered Accountant in Delhi who became my anchor during the flat sale. He was a master of his craft—guiding me through the nuances of property transactions, explaining capital gains, and breaking down the maze of short-term versus long-term tax implications. His calm confidence gave me the assurance I needed.

Then came **Pandey Ji**, my property agent in Indirapuram, Ghaziabad. The man knew the market like the back of his hand and handled the ground realities while I juggled deadlines and paperwork.

And how can I forget **Arvind Dubey** in Indirapuram, Ghaziabad, my dear friend? His hospitality was nothing short of lavish. His home became my base camp, and his family treated me like their own. **Seema**, his wife, was the perfect host, and their little daughter **Aavya**, just three years old, added a spark of innocence to those hectic days. Even **Shalini**, the full-time helper in their house, played her part in making my stay smooth.

Lastly, there was **Tapan Bhaiya** in Indirapuram, Ghaziabad and his family. He wasn't just a mentor; he was family. Our acquaintance goes back to 2006, the year I got married and moved into the very flat I was now here to sell. Over the years, he has been my guide on all financial matters, and during this trip, his advice was invaluable.

These people weren't just names on a list. They were the pillars that held me up when the weight of tasks threatened to pull me down. Without them, this journey would have been impossible.

CHAPTER 5

LANDING AND STAYING IN CHENNAI

I booked a cab inside the terminal and was relieved to find that I could pay with my international credit card. By the time we hit the road, it was almost 5 a.m. The city was waking up slowly—the streets were quiet, dotted with tea stalls where kettles hissed in the early dawn. The air carried that familiar mix of coastal breeze and Chennai humidity, and somewhere in the distance, I could hear the faint honk of autos and water tankers starting their day.

As we drove past empty flyovers and sleepy neighborhoods, I felt a strange calm. The sky was still coming out of the darkness and the smell of filter coffee wafted from roadside vendors preparing for the morning rush. It reminded me that I was home, yet not fully—an NRI with a mission, not a tourist.

I had already booked a hotel based on online reviews and trust me it was beyond my expectations. The check-in was smooth, the AC worked perfectly, and water bottles were waiting in the room. One small thing though—I wished the guy at the check-in counter had helped me drag my luggage from the elevator to my room. But never mind, I was in.

I changed clothes and tried to sleep, but sleep didn't come. My mind was racing—planning, prioritizing, wondering where to start. I had a big day ahead. My drop box appointment was scheduled for the next morning at 10 a.m., and before that, I needed passport-size photos.

Thankfully, I had exchanged some INR at Doha airport, so I had cash in my wallet. That was a relief because I had no active Indian debit or credit card, and international cards don't work everywhere.

The Wi-Fi worked, so I made a few WhatsApp calls to let my family in India and the USA know I had arrived and checked in. At some point, I dozed off. When I woke up, it was 9 am in the morning, and I headed straight for breakfast on the ground floor. Believe me, that was my first delightful moment in India—the menu had punnugulu, dosa, idli, sambhar vada and filter coffee. The aroma of fresh batter and sizzling ghee filled the air. I enjoyed every bite, thanked the staff, and went back to my room.

Jet lag hit me hard. I called Rupa and told her I couldn't even stand—my eyes were shutting on their own. Somehow, I woke up around 4 p.m., took bath , stepped out of the hotel and took an auto to a photo studio. **Delightful moment #2**—I got my photos in 10 minutes. The catch? I had to take 16 photos even though I needed only two. But all for 120 bucks—no complaints.

CHAPTER 6

SIM CARD SAGA AND THE GREAT ESCAPE

Since I had time, I thought of buying an Indian SIM and a phone to stay connected 24×7. Otherwise, I had to rely on Wi-Fi to make calls using my USA phone. After asking a few locals, I found a SIM shop and a mobile store nearby. I tried to act smart—first went to the SIM shop and explained my situation that I have no active document with an Indian address. Basically, nothing to satisfy KYC requirements for a new SIM .

The shopkeeper assured me, "Passport and NRI status? No problem, sir. You'll get the SIM."

Great! That sounded like music to my ears. So, I walked to the Phone shop next block and picked out a budget phone for ₹9,000. Nothing fancy—just something that could survive the hustle and my clumsy hands.

I told the guy at the phone shop, "Open the box, take out the SIM tray, and wait. I'll be back with the SIM from the nearby shop."

He nodded like a soldier receiving orders. And here's the kicker—I hadn't paid him yet. Not a single rupee.

As I walked away, I thought, *Wow, trust still exists in this world.* Or maybe he was just confident I'd return because his shop was the only one selling phones in a 500-meter radius. Either way, I felt like I was part of a social experiment on honesty.

I stepped out and headed back to the SIM shop, feeling like a man on a mission. This time, the shopkeeper decided to play tech wizard. He pulled out his phone and started filling out my application as an NRI, carefully typing in my USA address like he was writing a love letter.

Click. Error.

Try again. Error.

Third attempt? You guessed it—error.

After multiple tries, his confidence melted faster than ice cream in Chennai's heat. Finally, he sighed, looked at me, and said the words no customer wants to hear:

"Sir, system not accepting."

Now I am in trouble. The phone guy had already opened the box and was waiting for me like a groom at the mandap. And I hadn't paid him yet. My brain screamed, *Abort mission!*

I acted cool, flashed my best poker face, and told the SIM guy, "No worries, I'll check another shop and come back." He nodded, probably thinking I was a man of honor. Spoiler alert: I wasn't.

There was no other SIM shop nearby, and I had already walked far. So instead of going back, I hailed an auto and zipped straight to the hotel. Yes, I basically ghosted the phone guy. Cheated him? Maybe. But hey, not a big deal—he'll seal the box again and sell it to someone else.

Back at the hotel, I jumped straight into an office call. This was the first real test of my "work from India" plan. The call dragged on like a Netflix series with too many seasons, and by the time I hung up, it was 11:30 p.m.

I thought, *I'm in Chennai—surely I can grab some dinner outside.* Wrong assumption. The streets were silent, shutters down, like the city had collectively decided to fast. No way I was sleeping hungry.

Plan B: Swiggy. Ordered a veg thali from Saravana Bhavan using my international credit card—thank God for global fintech. When the food arrived, it felt like a rescue mission was completed. The aroma of sambar and chutney along with the masala dosa was pure comfort. I ate like a man who had just survived a famine.

After dinner, I stepped out for a breath of fresh air. Chennai night was warm. Back in my room, I checked the documents for the visa office visit next morning—passport, appointment letter, supporting papers—all laid out like soldiers ready for inspection.

Finally, I collapsed on the bed. Exhaustion hit me like a wave. Day one in India had been a cocktail of wins and lessons—a reminder that even the simplest tasks can turn into adventures when you're an NRI trying to reconnect with your roots.

Tomorrow is going to be big. Bigger than today. And I had no idea what surprises were waiting.

CHAPTER 7

THE DROP BOX AND JOURNEY TO BANGALORE

The next morning, I woke up a little anxious. Today was big—an important task was waiting, and there was no room for error. By 8:30 a.m., I had finished my breakfast, packed my documents like a soldier prepping for battle, and booked a cab to the U.S. Visa drop box center at Anna Salai.

The ride through Chennai's one-way streets was surprisingly smooth. The city was already buzzing—autos honking like they were part of a chaotic symphony, office-goers rushing as if late for a rocket launch, and the irresistible aroma of filter coffee drifting from roadside stalls. For a moment, I wished I could ditch the cab and grab a steel tumbler of that coffee, but duty called.

As we cruised past colonial-era buildings and shiny glass towers, I felt a strange mix of calm and anticipation. My mind replayed the checklist: passport, acknowledgment slip, ID proof—check, check, check. Still, a tiny voice whispered, *What if something goes wrong?* I silenced it with a deep breath and stared out at Chennai's morning hustle—a city that somehow balances tradition and chaos like a tightrope walker.

I reached the center on time. Medium traffic, nothing dramatic. The process inside was quick—barely 20 minutes. The guy at the counter verified my documents, smiled, and said, "All good." He explained when and how I could collect my stamped passport. That was one major task down. By 10:30 a.m., I was back in my hotel room, calling Rupa to share the good news.

After catching up on emails and WhatsApp messages, I checked out at noon and headed straight to Chennai Central. My brother-in-law Subrata, who works in Bangalore, had booked me on Shatabdi Express. The train was scheduled for 5:30 p.m., but I reached the station at 12:30 p.m. Now imagine this—I was standing at the entrance of Chennai Central with four pieces of luggage: two big suitcases, one carry-on, and a laptop bag with two laptops inside. That laptop bag was no joke—it felt like carrying bricks. If someone had asked me to run, I'd have applied for a Guinness World Record in "slow-motion sprint."

Two challenges stared at me in the face:

1. How to survive five hours in Chennai's humidity?
2. How to manage this mountain of luggage without turning into a porter myself?

I was swarmed by porters like bees spotting a sugar jar. Their eyes said it all: "***Bakra mil gaya. Aaj halal karenge*** (Like a lamb to the slaughter)" I could almost hear their mental calculators clicking away, estimating how much they could squeeze out of me.

Thankfully, my undergrad days at NIT Trichy came to the rescue. I remembered the station had a decent locker room—a lifesaver for travelers drowning in luggage. Back in college days we used to deposit our luggage here and spend time on Marina beach. Thanks to Raka Max our ringleader at that time. Without wasting time, I switched to negotiation mode.

"***Bhai, locker room le chalo. Tum log help karo, baaki main dekh lunga*** (Brother, take me to the locker room. You guys help with the luggage, I'll handle the rest.) ," I said, trying to sound confident while clutching my bags like they were family heirlooms.

We struck a deal. They carried my luggage on a cart like seasoned sherpas, weaving through the chaos of the station.

Finally, we reached the locker room—a dimly lit sanctuary with rows of metal boxes that looked older than my engineering textbooks. The porters helped me check in the bags and promised to return later to help me board the train. Sounded like a flawless plan. Or so I believed. I didn't pay them upfront—the deal was clear: payment after I was safely on board.

As I locked the last bag and pocketed the deposit slip, a wave of relief washed over me. For the first time that day, I felt light—literally and figuratively. Little did I know, this was just the calm before the next storm.

With the luggage sorted, I needed a place to kill time. And where there's a will, there's a way—I spotted a lounge. The rates were steep, but worth every rupee for air conditioning. The guy at the desk asked for a photo ID, and my old PAN card from 2002 came to the rescue. Remember, my passport was deposited at the drop box earlier that morning. *More incomplete now,* I thought with a grin.

I spent the next four hours in the lounge, catching my breath under the AC, pretending to be a business traveler while secretly binge-scrolling memes. When the train finally arrived, the porter showed up as promised. Boarding with all that luggage was still a workout, and in the process, I accidentally stepped on a lady's foot. She winced in pain—I apologized quickly and moved on, silently praying she wouldn't curse me in Tamil.

The Shatabdi pulled out on time. As the train sped toward Bangalore, I gazed out the window, watching the changing landscape—lush fields, small towns, and the occasional temple dome peeking through the greenery. Bangalore had been home for years, and I couldn't help but notice how much had changed. Yet, one thing hadn't—the weather. Pleasant as always.

We reached Bangalore around 10 p.m. My cousin Anshuman was still on the road, so I waited outside the station, tired but relieved. When I finally got home, I switched on my phone—it only worked on Wi-Fi—and saw multiple missed calls from my super boss. That was unusual. I called him back, and he picked up immediately. We spoke briefly—he wanted to pitch me for a new assignment and asked for my updated CV.

Back to reality. Anshu walked in holding a kadai of chicken cooked in mustard oil—Bihari/Odiya style, thanks to Ramakant, his cook from Odisha. He had gone the extra mile because he thought, *My bhaiya is coming—let's make something special.* I felt bad when I told him I couldn't eat non-veg during the holy Shravan month. He looked disappointed, but that's Anshu—no love lost between us.

Rupa has two relationships with Anshu—she's his Masi and also his Bhabhi. Bhabhi from my side, of course. Family ties like these make life interesting.

As I sat at the dinner table with a simple vegetarian meal, I thought about the day. From the drop box relief to the chaos of Chennai Central, to the warmth of family in Bangalore—it had been a roller coaster. And tomorrow? Tomorrow was going to be even bigger.

CHAPTER 8

MY STAY IN BANGALORE AND THE CONTROLLED CHAOS

Anshu is twenty-seven or twenty-eight, very much a bachelor—and his apartment showed every sign of it. The moment I stepped in, I felt like I had entered a live episode of *Bachelor Pad Chronicles*. Dusting, I realized, was probably at the very bottom of his priority list (pun fully intended). I couldn't help but compare his lifestyle to my bachelor days. At least back then, I tried to keep my room somewhat organized and dust-free. Anshu clearly had other ambitions—Bikes, Netflix and gaming, not cleaning.

That first night in Bangalore didn't go as planned. I suddenly came down with fever and found myself shivering in his two-bedroom apartment. I started scrambling for anything that could act as a blanket—bedsheets, sofa throws, maybe even curtains if it came to that. I piled them all on top of me, but the shivering refused to stop. I suspected it was because of the constant switch between the cool blast of the AC and the daytime heat of the sun. My body was staging a protest.

After suffering in silence for some time, I finally decided it was no use struggling alone. I called out to Anshu, who was fast asleep in the other room. Half-asleep, he stumbled like a zombie.

Me: "Do you have any paracetamol?"

Anshu: (rubbing his eyes) "Yeah… somewhere… wait."

Fever management first—diagnosis later. Thankfully, he had a strip of tablets. I popped one and managed to doze off for a while.

But once the medicine wore off, the fever came roaring back like an uninvited guest. Time for real action. I picked up the phone and called my cousin Subrata, who also happens to be my brother-in-law, married to Rupa's youngest sister. He's not an MBBS doctor, but in family circles, his medical advice is treated with great respect—and rightly so.

Me: "Subrata, fever's back Bro. What do I do?"

Subrata: "Start a proper course of medication. I'll send you the names."

One of the best things about India? The ease of access to medicines. No prescription drama—just head to a pharmacy and ask. I sent Anshu out with a list of medicines. Within the hour, I had my first dose, and soon the fever began to settle down. Crisis averted.

The next morning, with energy slowly coming back, I turned my attention to the tasks I had in Bangalore. First on the list was collecting some important property documents from HDFC Bank. For that, I needed to carry an ID proof, and as I had mentioned earlier, the only valid one I had was my good old PAN card.

But I also needed a xerox copy of it. I casually asked Anshu:

Me: "Is there a Xerox shop nearby?"

Anshu: (grinning) "Why step out? Just order it on Blinkit."

Me: "Order a photocopy online? Are you kidding?"

Anshu: "Upload the document. Ten minutes later, it's at your doorstep."

My mind was blown. India had moved ahead while I was stuck in nostalgia lane.

Armed with my PAN Xerox, we set out for the bank. We tried taking some inner alleys to dodge Bangalore's notorious traffic, but there's only so much you can avoid. Finally, we reached, only to be told:

Bank Staff: "Sir, these documents are at the main branch. You need to give advance notice."

After all the effort, I had to return empty-handed. *More incomplete now,* I thought, laughing at my luck.

On the way back, we decided to make a detour and check on Anand's under construction apartment. Anand, Anshu's flat mate in that dusty house, was currently in Mumbai nursing a knee injury. Little did I know that this short trip would turn into a full-on test of patience and endurance—Bangalore traffic style.

As soon as we hit the main roads, it became clear that moving forward would be a lesson in frustration. Traffic in Bangalore doesn't just crawl—it meditates. Sometimes, it seems to disappear entirely, leaving you stranded while the chaos hums around you. More often than moving, we were standing still, inching forward in bursts that lasted barely a few meters. Riding pillion, I could feel my back stiffening and protesting. Every bump, every sudden stop, was a small reminder that my body was still recovering from the previous day's fever.

While inching along, my eyes inevitably wandered to the numerous biryani points lining the streets. Each shop claimed it had the "best biryani in Bangalore," with steaming platters of chicken, mutton, and vegetable biryanis on display. The aroma was tempting, but honestly, I had zero appetite. My mood was more geared toward surviving the traffic than sampling local delicacies, so I ignored the tantalizing smells and kept my focus on the road ahead.

After what felt like an eternity, we finally reached Anand's under-construction flat. The property itself was impressive—a solid structure with good spacing and a promising layout. It was tucked quite far from the main road, nestled into the interior of the neighborhood. The location was peaceful, but I couldn't help but think about the commute anyone living there would face every day. After a brief look, we turned back, ready to tackle the return journey.

And then came the surprise. On the way back, I saw something that almost made me gasp: bike riders were using the footpath as their personal express lane, racing ahead to beat the traffic.

Me: "Are you seeing this?!"

Anshu: (laughing) "Welcome to Bangalore, bhaiya."

It was audacious, almost cinematic, yet terrifying to watch. Cars, pedestrians, and these footpath racers seemed to coexist in some chaotic harmony that only Bangalore could manage. We didn't dare follow suit; safety first. I hung on tighter, bracing myself for the slow, steady crawl back through the city streets.

By the time we finally returned, my back ached, patience had been tested, and my admiration for those who navigated this madness daily had grown exponentially. Bangalore had already started showing me its quirks—the unpredictability, the audacity, and the small, often humorous, little rules that everyone seemed to bend in their own favor.

It wasn't a productive day in terms of tasks, but it was already shaping up to be a memorable one in terms of experiences

CHAPTER 9

MEETING WITH MY NIECE AND FLYING TO RANCHI

By late afternoon after taking a nap and another round of medicine , I was feeling better .My next stop was Deepa and Subrata's place—and of course, to see my little niece, Anira. She's the star of the house, and the way she calls me **"Mausa Ji"** always makes me feel like a celebrity.

Their home is in RR Nagar, and honestly, I like that side of Bangalore far more than Whitefield. It's calmer, greener, and doesn't have that rushed, suffocating vibe of the tech-heavy areas. The cab ride itself felt like a luxury—just sitting back and letting someone else battle the traffic was pure bliss.

On the way, Anshu and I caught up. The conversation, as usual, drifted toward marriage and this generation's hesitation about it.

Me: "So, any plans yet?"

Anshu: (laughing) "Plans? Bhaiya, marriage is like a software update—everyone fears it'll slow down their system."

Me: "True. And no one reads the terms and conditions."

We laughed, but beneath the jokes was a quiet realization—times have changed. This generation is shying away from that commitment.

After about ninety minutes, we reached Subrata's place and to be greeted by the security guards at the entrance. After punching the visitor details, we were allowed inside. Anira was waiting at the door, bouncing with excitement. That smile on her face was enough to wash away the fatigue of travel and my illness.

Anira: "Mausa Ji! You came!"

Me: "Of course! Who else will play cricket with you in the drawing room?"

I thanked Subrata for the "magic pills" that had saved me from fever and checked on Deepa, who wasn't feeling too well.She was five months pregnant. Then Anira pulled me straight into her world—first a game of cricket right in the living room, then some help with her homework. She's sharp, but her energy is endless. Honestly, I was struggling to keep up.

Dinner was simple, family-style. While eating, we put on **"Taarak Mehta Ka Ooltah Chashmah."** It's funny how quickly you slip into that comfort zone with family—you don't even notice time passing.

The next morning, I woke up to a scene straight out of a sitcom—Deepa instructing Subrata on how to do pochha (mopping). Subrata was taking great care of Deepa and helping her with the daily chores.

Deepa: "Straight lines, Subrata! Not zig-zag!"

Subrata: (muttering) "Yes, ma'am…"

I couldn't help smiling. By the time I stepped out of the bed , the whole place was sparkling clean. The maid had taken leave, so they had stepped into her shoes for the day.

Since my flight to Ranchi was in the afternoon, I had a few hours to spare. Anira insisted on chocolates, so we headed to a nearby mall. It was crowded with weekend shoppers, but the bustle felt oddly refreshing after the quiet routines of my US life. A bit of noise and chaos can sometimes feel comforting.

Back at their place, I had lunch, packed up, and got ready to leave. Anshu dropped me at the airport, and that was the last I saw of him on this trip.

As I walked toward security, Anira's voice still echoed in my ears:

Anira: "Mausa Ji, next time bring Anusha Didi from America!". Anusha is my younger daughter.

Me: "Deal!"

With goodbyes done and a heart full of family warmth, I headed toward the next chapter of my journey, Ranchi. Ranchi here I come my darling.

CHAPTER 10

WELCOME TO RANCHI

Welcome with rain—that's how Ranchi greeted me. Titu, my younger brother, and Akshu, his son and my nephew, came to receive me at the Birsa Munda Airport . The airport sits in **Hinoo**, just about 5–7 km from the city center, and it's surprisingly modern for a Tier-II city. The integrated terminal, inaugurated in 2013, has a clean, compact design that makes navigation easy—no endless walking like in big metros. No marathon walks here—just a short sprint to baggage claim. It's small but efficient—perfect for a quick entry into Ranchi without the stress of sprawling terminals.

Inside, you'll find **escalators, free Wi-Fi, lounges and even tribal artwork** that gives the place a local flavor. There are small restaurants serving snacks, mobile charging points, and a childcare room for families. If you're early, you can relax in the lounge or browse through souvenir shops showcasing Jharkhand's crafts.

The vibe is calm compared to the chaos of bigger airports. Security checks are straightforward, and prepaid taxi counters and Ola/Uber kiosks make getting out hassle-free. Outside, the air smells fresh after rain.

The whole way back home, the rain kept us company, tapping on the windshield like an old friend. As we drove through familiar streets, I couldn't help reminiscing about my old days in this area—especially Hinoo. We used to walk that route sometimes, or at least half of it. From Kusai Colony to Kilburn or maybe Shukla Colony… or was it somewhere else? Honestly, my memory was playing tricks. *Forget it,* I told myself with a smile.

The moment I reached home, the first thing I did was touch my parents' feet. That ritual never gets old. Soon after, came the tea—without sugar, of course. Mom and Ruma (my sister in law) already knew my preference. That feeling? Eternal.

My dad, **Binoy Kumar Jha**, lovingly called **Godu**, is 83 years old. He retired in 2002 (the year I joined my first job as a software Engineer in Wipro after graduating as an Industrial Engineer from NIT, Trichy). He retired as head clerk from Bihar Electricity board. He mostly stays at home and occasionally go outside. He charges his battery by getting involved in everything happening in the house. Asking annoying questions (pun intended), giving suggestions—basically, keeping himself busy.

Dad: "So, how was the flight? Did you eat anything?"

Me: "Yes, Baba. All good."

He's everywhere in the house, and honestly, I love that about him. Simple at heart, and wonderful singer. This time, we even discussed old songs, and he sang a few lines of Manna Dey, that were pure magic.

Mom, **Urvashi Devi**, is in her mid-70s—the real head of the family. I don't want this to sound like a tribute, but let me just say: *I love you, Mom.* She's still active, waking up at 5:30 a.m. sharp. Her chela aka follower, Ruma, follows soon after, and together they start the day with tea. Then Mom heads out to get milk from the nearby **khatal (cow sheds)**.

One day, Titu suggested:

Titu: "Why don't we just use packet milk? It'll save you the trouble."

Mom just smiled. Change isn't easy when habits are decades old.

Titu, my brother, is what I call a street-smart **jugaadu**. He has connections everywhere. I applied for my voter ID card sitting at home, and five days later, the new card was in my hand. That's Titu for you.

So here I was, with half my family in Ranchi and the other half in the USA. And through all this, I was still working U.S. hours because I couldn't plan PTO. Imagine sitting in Ranchi, sipping tea, and attending late-night calls. *Global citizen problems,* right?

CHAPTER 11

STAY PART 1 IN RANCHI

The next morning, the mission was clear: visit the Aadhaar office and apply for my Aadhaar card. This was the first step in my journey from **Incomplete NRI** to **Complete NRI**.

I gathered the courage to go, remembering my last visit during Holi last year—queues snaking from the ground floor to the second floor. This time? No different. People clutching forms, waiting for their turn, faces etched with patience and frustration.

Looking at the scene, I wasn't sure if joining the queue would get me anywhere today. So, I walked up to the security guard managing the crowd.

Me: "Bhaiya, can I go upstairs? Just want to check if my documents are complete."

Security: (after a pause) "Theek hai, jao."

Upstairs, the processing center was a sea of people. Employees looked overwhelmed, juggling forms and queries. I scanned the room and spotted a board: **Validation Personnel**. Perfect. I approached the guy.

Me: "Sir, can you check my documents?"

Validation Guy: (without looking up) "Busy right now."

Not his fault—he was drowning in work. I realized waiting here was pointless. This was the main center handling new applications, and smaller centers don't entertain fresh cases.

I stepped into the corridor, hoping for a miracle—or at least someone willing to help for a "convenience fee." A pamphlet caught my eye: **Book Online Appointment**. Great idea, except the link refused to work on my phone (borrowed from my sister-in-law). My personal phone only works on wi-fi in India so her phone was my life line for few days.

While fiddling with the link, I noticed a room where three men were surrounded by applicants. They seemed to be helping with forms and online bookings. I approached one of them and explained my situation. At first, he barely listened—until I said:

Me: "I need to apply for Aadhaar for myself. I'm 48."

Helper: (eyes widening) "You don't have Aadhaar?!"

He thought I was applying for my kid. I explained:

Me: "Been outside India for 12–13 years. Never got the chance. My wife told me to apply during the drive in 2017. I ignored it. My fault."

He nodded, then broke the bad news:

Helper: "PAN card works for ID and DOB, but you need address proof. Passport has U.S. address, ration card outdated, DL expired… tough case."

He suggested starting with a voter ID application and when that is issued I can use that as my address proof in India. I took his number and promised to call later.

Walking out of that crowded building, I felt a mix of relief and frustration. At least I had directions now.

Back home, I shared the story with Titu. Later in the evening, I called that guy—no answer. Left a WhatsApp message. He called back around 9 p.m.

Aadhar office Guy: "Apply voter ID with your parents' address."

I handed my PAN copy to Titu and he sent to one of his friend and with Dad's Aadhaar number, the application was submitted online.

Titu: "Ho gaya. Fifteen days and you can download it online."

Easy peasy.

Feeling lighter, I decided to pamper myself early next morning—a haircut and massage at the local salon across the road. My house is barely 100 meters from the main road. But God had other plans. It was Tuesday—Lord Hanuman's day—and most salons were closed. Determined, I headed to Doranda Bazaar, especially the Muslim mohalla. My guess was right—the first salon I saw was open. It wasn't fancy—an 8x8 shop with two chairs. One was occupied, so I waited. Nostalgia hit hard. This was the same area where we bought quota ration—sugar and kerosene—in the late '80s. LPG was a luxury then; home delivery was a distant dream.

The salon guy was a decent professional. While trimming my hair, we chatted.

Me: "You've been here long?"

Salon Guy: "Born and raised. This shop's been here for years." I shared by feelings of nostalgia with him and he was able to relate with it.

I walked out feeling lighter—both in weight and mood. That haircut wasn't just grooming; it was a reconnection with my roots.

Back home, I slipped into work mode for U.S. hours, juggling calls and emails. Meanwhile, my next big mission loomed: **Mission Registry on 14th August**.

Before I wrap this chapter, a quick flashback: life in India before moving to the U.S. in 2012. I worked at CSC Noida, lived near Shipra Mall, Ghaziabad. In 2010, I switched to Accenture and moved to Bangalore. Our Ghaziabad flat was rented out for 15 years. Now, almost 20 years old, it showed signs of wear and tear. Out of sight, out of mind—and now, the plan was to sell it.

CHAPTER 12

PROJECT RAKSHA BANDHAN

How can I forget to tell you about my Raksha Bandhan project? If you're traveling to India and staying for a few weeks, you're bound to bump into one or two festivals. I was lucky this time—I got to celebrate Raksha Bandhan in person, not virtually. Real hugs, real sweets, real chaos.

I landed in Ranchi on the 2nd of August, and the festival was on the 9th. So here was the plan: I told my mom, "Anyway, I have to go to Bokaro to meet my sisters and cousins. Why not leave a day earlier, visit my in-laws in Chas, and stay overnight? Next day, Titu—my younger brother—will drive to Bokaro for Raksha Bandhan(he does it every year) and I'll hitch a ride back to Ranchi with him." Mom nodded. Plan approved.

On the 8th,my brother dropped me to Ranchi Railway Station and I boarded the Shatabdi from Ranchi to Howrah via Bokaro. The journey was smooth except for one minor detail—I got a free subscription to other people's business in my coach. Some folks were talking so loudly on their phones that I now know their quarterly targets and family drama. Public speaking is a skill, but public whispering? That's an art we still need to learn.

And then came the "audio version" of *Son of Sardaar Part 2.* A gentleman in the next row decided to watch the movie and headphones were optional. So, the entire coach willingly or unwillingly enjoyed the movie—whether they wanted to or not. I swear, half the junta was in the same boat.

The train reached Bokaro Steel City Junction (yes, it's a junction) ahead of time. I hopped off, expecting no grand welcome because I hadn't told anyone my arrival details. Booked an auto after some classic mol-molai (bargaining). Managed a discount of 50 bucks—just over half a dollar—but still felt like I'd won a war. One condition though: the auto guy had to stop at a sweet shop. You don't show up at your sasural empty-handed. Rupa would do *line-haazir(take class)* on me if I dared. The auto driver suggested buying sweets near the station since we'd take the bypass road. Smart man. I agreed.

Forty-five minutes later, I reached my in-laws' place. Quick background: my father-in-law is around 80, mother-in-law about 70. They live alone, though a maid helps with chores, and Rupa's eldest sister—my mami too—lives nearby and checks in often.

The auto dropped me at the gate. I knocked on the iron door (that's an art too). My father-in-law opened it with a warm smile. Mom-in-law was inside, busy making refreshments. I touched their feet, took blessings, and settled on the couch for a quick catch-up.

It was almost 5 PM, and I had office work starting at 7, so no big plans. While sipping tea, I gazed out the window. The guavas on the tree caught my eye. I dragged my MIL outside, plucked a few, washed them, and asked for a plate with salt. Pure bliss—fresh guavas with a pinch of salt. But nothing comes free. The mosquitoes on that tree had a feast on me. By the time I came back, I was itching like crazy. Asked MIL for coconut oil and applied it generously. It took 30 minutes for the irritation to calm down. Lesson learned: guavas are sweet, but mosquitoes are sweeter on you.

Dinner was simple, conversation warm. After that, I slipped into work mode. Nothing dramatic, just a quiet evening in Chas.

CHAPTER 13

THE RAKHI DAY

Next morning was Raksha Bandhan. I called Titu, my younger brother, who was supposed to start from Ranchi and head to Chas, near my in-law's place, for the celebration at our elder sister's house.

Me: "Where are you now?"

Titu: "Relax, I'll be there in one and a half hours max."

I got ready, picked up some sweets from a nearby grocery store, and walked to my eldest sister's house—it's just a short distance away. My brother-in-law, Mr. Prakash, was outside doing something.

Me: "Namaste, Jiju!"

Jiju: "Arre, Kutu! Come in, come in." Kutu is my nickname.

I went upstairs to meet Didi. We caught up over tea and waited for Titu. He arrived after a while, and the Rakhi ceremony began. The ritual itself is simple yet profound. Sisters prepare a **thali**—a decorated plate with a rakhi, rice grains, a small diya, and sweets. The rakhi isn't just a thread; it's a promise. She ties it on her brother's wrist, applies a **tilak** on his forehead, and whispers a silent prayer for his well-being. In return, the brother vows to protect her. We stood close, smiling, feeling that bond renew itself.

Me and Titu had already collaborated to buy a beautiful saree for Didi. We handed it over and touched her feet for blessings. Jiju played the official photographer, capturing every moment. That's what Raksha

Bandhan is—a yearly renewal of an unspoken contract. And this time, I was physically present to sign it. (Just kidding!).

Lunch followed. Midway, someone joined us, and the conversation drifted to ground-level political realities and the current situation in Jharkhand and West Bengal. Nothing like spicy debates with spicy food.

CHAPTER 14

SECOND STOP: CHIRA CHAS

Next, I headed to my younger sister's house in Chira Chas, a urban residential colony in close proximity of Bokaro. She lives with her two sons, in-laws, and of course, my brother-in-law Rakesh. Arnav, the elder nephew, is twelve and a foodie. So, I made sure to bring his favorite rasgullas. Ishu, the younger one, is nine and obsessed with cricket. He's even taking coaching.

I had once joked on the phone:

Me: "Your Mamajee was a good spin bowler in his time. I'll bowl to you someday."

He remembered that. So, after the Rakhi ceremony and lunch, Ishu dragged me downstairs to the badminton court, where a few of his friends were waiting.

Ishu (to his friends): "This is my Mamajee. He's a spin bowler!"

Me: "Okay, you bat, I'll bowl."

We were using a tennis ball so the security guard, after initial hesitation gave us permission to play in the badminton court. We have to be careful as buildings glassed were exposed to the court. But poor Ishu didn't get to bat first—his uncle, Prateek Ji, was visiting because his wife was tying Rakhi to Rakesh. Prateek Ji grabbed the bat and started showing off his batting skills.

I bowled leg-spin, my specialty. Beat him once and almost got him stumped—except there was no wicketkeeper. He hit a couple of classy drives though. Eventually, Ishu and Arnav got their turns. Honestly, Ishu's bowling impressed me more than his batting. At that age, on concrete turf, he was swinging the ball!

CHAPTER 15

THE RAINY TWIST

By 4 PM, we bid goodbye and headed to my cousin sister Archana's house, about 4–5 km away. I was meeting with her after so many years. This was our final stop before me and my brother head back to Ranchi. As soon as we left the society and crossed a mini stream (*naala*), the rain came down like someone had turned on a giant shower. The wipers started their rhythmic dance—except one blade was acting like a rebel, flapping awkwardly and threatening to snap off. Luckily, we were near Sector 4 market.

Titu: "Don't worry, I know a car decor shop nearby."

I nodded. We reached the shop in pouring rain. I stayed in the car while Titu spoke to the owner. Turns out, the owner knew him—Titu was his medical insurance agent, referred by Rakesh. That bond paid off. When Titu asked for the charge after fixing the wiper, the owner refused.

Owner: "Arre, no need. You're family."

Titu: "No, no, take it."

Finally, he accepted. I got introduced too and we continued to Archana's place.

Archana is my maternal uncle's daughter. We were close during my Class 10 days, but life happened—high school, engineering prep—and visits became rare. Raksha Bandhan gave us a chance to reconnect. I learned about her son, a prodigy being coached for IITs by a premier institute in Chandigarh on a full ride. Amazing!

This was only my second visit to her in-laws' place, now her home. We spent over an hour chatting, did the rakhi ritual, handed over gifts, and enjoyed tea and refreshments. She served **dahi bada**—South Indian style with curry leaves and mustard seeds. Though I was stuffed from earlier feasts, I savored it.

CHAPTER 16

THE DRIVE BACK

We left for Ranchi around 6 PM. The drive was smooth, except for a few stretches where I admired Titu's driving skills. It was still poring , so I kept asking:

Me: "Can you see the road ahead?"

Titu (grinning): "Of course. Don't worry, I've driven in worse."

I wasn't convinced. The headlights were weak, barely slicing through the sheets of rain. He maneuvered like a pro, even as water gushed along the sides of the road.

He assured me every time. On the Sikindiri stretch, I spotted a temporary temple—*Baba Barfani*—built near a natural stream. In the night calm, the gurgling water was unmissable and loud, like nature whispering secrets. Titu had a steering knob that helped him maneuver the ghats. Inside, the dashboard lights glowed soft green, casting shadows on Titu's focused face. I kept checking the road ahead, but honestly, I was admiring his skill more than worrying. Three hours later, we rolled into Ranchi, tired but content.

We reached home by 10 PM. I gave Mom the full update—where we went first, what food was served, whether the sisters liked the sarees, and yes, whether I warmed up the nephews with cricket. Had tea, then dinner, and called it a day. Honestly, I don't even remember if it was a weekday or weekend—did I work or take PTO? No clue.

CHAPTER 17

TRIP TO DELHI – MISSION REGISTRY

This is where the Delhi cohort enters the story. The first person? The quintessential **Pandey ji**, my property agent. He had already arranged a buyer, and I agreed to the amount and the buyer's profile. The deal was informally signed, and the token money was transferred even before I booked my India travel. So far, so good.

But the real challenge was **Mission Registry**, which depended entirely on **Mission Drop Box**—my visa stamping appointment. Without that, nothing else could move. By God's grace that mission is accomplished without any ask for additional documents (I was proud of my due diligence on that in that short time. *Little self-praise.*) and now my stamped passport is in Delhi VAC center and ready to be picked any day. My return flight to the U.S. was on **17th August**, early morning. That meant I had until **16th evening** to wrap everything up and head to the airport. One sacrifice was already clear: celebrating my birthday on the plane alone. Yes, **16th August** is my birthday.

Coming back to the main track, Mission Registry was locked for **14th August**. But there were prerequisites. I was still in Ranchi recovering from all the travel stress and enjoying homemade delicacies when the second person in the Delhi cohort called—**Arvind**, my CA. He was handling the low TDS certificate, which was crucial before registration. The buyer had to pay TDS and show it to the bank for loan disbursement.

The buyer can only pay the TDS once he knows the amount and Arvind CA was confirming the amount with the IT department. I was learning the stuff.

I picked up his call. Yes my phone was working as I was on my home wi-fi.

“Sir, we have a problem,” Arvind said.

“Problem? Don’t tell me the certificate is delayed,” I replied.

“Not just delayed. Your PAN is inoperative. We can’t apply for TDS until that’s fixed.”

That was a bummer. It was already **8th August**, and D-Day was **14th**. My plan was to travel to Delhi on **Sunday, the 10th**. I had given heads up to my manager that I might need to extend my stay by a week if things went south. And now, they were going south.

Enter person three and four in the Delhi cohort—**Tapan Singh**, my go-to advisor for anything and everything, and **Arvind**, my friend and host in Delhi. I told them, “Guys, 14th looks impossible now. No TDS certificate, and now this PAN mess. I’m thinking of extending my stay.”

Both replied in chorus:

“Hold on. Don’t tell Pandey ji or the CA yet. Keep the intensity. Act like 14th is still the target.”

Why was my PAN inoperative? Because it wasn’t linked to Aadhaar. And why wasn’t it linked? Because I never applied for Aadhaar. Classic NRI problem.

I called Arvind (the CA) back:

“How do we get out of this catch-22?”

"Sir, we'll update your status on the Income Tax portal from Resident to NRI. That removes the Aadhaar dependency."

"Great. What do you need?"

"All your passport stampings and U.S. address proof."This will establish my NRI status.

Easy—except my passport was sitting at the Delhi VAC center post visa stamping. For a moment, it felt like the light at the end of the tunnel had gone out. Then I remembered—I had soft copies of everything. After digging through old emails, I found the attachments and sent them to Arvind immediately. He submitted the application and promised movement by tomorrow.

On **9th morning**, I called Arvind again.

"Any update?"

"Sir, I'll confirm by afternoon."

That afternoon, he called back:

"PAN is active now. Hurray!"

He explained that he had to send one of his office guys with the documents to expedite the process. The conveyance allowance for that guy was more than renting a seven-star cab, but at this point, time was more precious than money.

With that sorted, I booked my flight to Delhi. Mission Registry was back on track for **14th August**. I felt a strange mix of relief and tension. One hurdle was cleared—the PAN was active, the visa stamped—but the real test was yet to come. **Mission Registry** was still looming like a final boss in a video game. Would Pandey ji pull it off? Would the paperwork dance go smoothly? Or would Delhi throw in a last-minute twist?

The next few days were going to decide whether I celebrated my birthday on a plane with a smile—or with unfinished business haunting me at 30,000 feet.

The day was August 10th, and my flight to Delhi was at 6 PM. The plan was simple—Titu would drop me at Birsa Munda Airport, and from there, the journey to the capital would begin. But inside, it wasn't simple at all. My mind was buzzing with excitement, a little anxiety, and that strange feeling you get when you're leaving a familiar place for a city that never sleeps.

The afternoon in Ranchi was calm. I did the usual pre-travel ritual—checking my bag for the charger, wallet, and ID for the fifth time. Why do we do that even after packing everything the night before? Maybe it's the traveler's paranoia. I knew I'd miss this quiet once I hit Delhi's chaos. But that's the thrill—two worlds, two rhythms, and I was the bridge for today.

Titu arrived, and we loaded the bags into his car. The drive to the airport was short. My mind was racing faster than the car. At the airport, the usual drill—security checks, boarding pass, and that moment when you finally sit near the gate and breathe. I grabbed a coffee, not because I needed it, but because airports make you crave coffee. Watching people rush around with their trolley bags, I felt that familiar traveler's excitement. It's like everyone has a story, and for a few hours, all those stories share the same space.

Actually, the coffee had its own story. I was craving it, so I looked around and saw a Nescafé counter near my boarding gate. I walked up and asked the guy about the options. He silently pointed to the menu on his left. I glanced at it—and froze. Nothing under ₹250. My mind started debating: *Should I really spend that much on a small cup of coffee?* Sugar wasn't the problem. The problem was my mental block about paying that much for coffee.

Meanwhile, people around me were buying coffee and tea without a second thought. That's when I told myself:

Me (to myself): "It's okay, bro. It's the airport. Things will be costly. This isn't the India you left years ago. This is the new India—people live to earn and enjoy, not just earn and save."

With that pep talk, I paid the price and got my coffee. Walked to an empty chair and took a sip. Oh my God—the sugar hit me like a punch. For the last couple of years, I've avoided raw sugar completely, and this cup was loaded. I wanted to trash it immediately, but then another voice in my head said:

Mind: "Don't waste ₹250. That's money down the drain."

So I kept sipping, punishing myself with every sweet gulp. Finally, I convinced my mind:

Me: "Enough. This is torture."

And I trashed the coffee. Lesson learned—sometimes, letting go is cheaper than forcing yourself.

As I walked toward the boarding gate, I smiled. This little coffee episode was a reminder of how much India has changed—and how much I've changed too. The flight was about to board, and I was ready for the next chapter of this journey.

CHAPTER 18

GATE NO. 3 AND THE PINK DRESS

Landed in Delhi around 8 PM. Picked up a box of sweets for Arvind bhai and his family from Haldiram's outlet inside the Terminal before stepping out of the arrival gate. Booked a cab from the Delhi Police counter—smooth process, no drama.

It felt good to be back after years. Delhi was buzzing, restless as ever. New billboards, shiny car models, hawkers reshaping the streets—everything screamed change. From the cab window, the city looked like it was sprinting ahead without waiting for anyone.

Reached Arvind bhai's place by 11:30 PM. His community, ATS Advantage, has five entry and exit gates. His block is 10, closest to Gate No. 3. But visitors can't enter by car through that gate unless they're ready for extra paperwork and drama. I wasn't. So I got down at Gate 3 leaving the cab and dragged my luggage to his tower.

By the time I signed the register in the lobby, I was panting. **Reality check:** I'm getting old. Took the lift to the 8th floor and rang the bell, expecting a sleepy household.

Wrong assumption. The door opened, and his three-year-old daughter, Avya, ran straight into my arms. She knew I was coming and was clearly excited. Handed the sweets to Seema (Arvind's wife) and sank into a bean bag. Aavya wasn't letting me talk to anyone else—she wanted full attention.

I asked her to come along to the room where Arvind had placed my luggage—my den for the next few days. Opened a bag and pulled out the dress I'd bought for her in Ranchi. She took one look, dropped it on the floor, and declared:

"I only like pink."

To make matters worse, I'd guessed her size wrong. One size short. Promised her a pink dress next time. She played with me for a while before Shalini, the full-time caretaker, took her to bed after feeding her. The storm had passed.

Caught up with Arvind and Seema, shared updates, and discussed plans for the next few days. Dinner? Honestly, I don't remember the main course. What I do remember: **masala papad, peanut masala, and the single malt I'd picked up at Doha Duty Free for Arvind.**

Arvind didn't join me for the drink—stomach issues and he was on antibiotics. But the conversation flowed. We touched on everything from geopolitics to government inefficiency. One line from him stuck:

"You were in that cab for one and a half hours. Did you see any government employee working?"

That hit me. His point: the system is broken. Taxes are collected, but work on the ground? Minimal. I kept observing that during my entire stay.

It was Sunday, so no office work to worry about. Just Delhi, old friends, and thoughts that lingered.

CHAPTER 19

THE CHASE BEGINS -GET SET AND GO

I woke up the next morning with a mental checklist that looked more like a battleground. First call of the day? Pandey ji, my property Agent. I had already informed him that I was in Delhi and promised to meet him in front of Amrapali Green Society later where I have my flat. That flat—my house—had been on rent for fifteen years. Fifteen years of someone else's curtains, someone else's tea stains, someone else's life. And now, it was time to reclaim it.

The tenant had been given a heads-up weeks ago: I had a buyer(Gaurav) and he needed to vacate by the 15th of August. Initially, the plan was relaxed—last week of August, plenty of time. But then came the twist. The buyer, Gaurav, wanted the keys by the evening of the 13th. Suddenly, my calendar looked like a ticking bomb.

I called the tenant, explained the situation, and braced for resistance. Sure enough, it came—polite but firm.

"Weekdays, sir… it's difficult to vacate on such short notice. I had planned my logistics based on the earlier deadline—last week of this month," he said, his voice carrying the weight of Delhi's classic excuses. I could almost picture him shaking his head dramatically, like a Bollywood hero refusing a villain's offer.

Inside, I groaned. This was the kind of curveball that makes you question every life decision, including why you didn't just become a monk in the Himalayas. But I wasn't giving up. I switched to my best negotiation mode—the one that sounds like empathy but smells like desperation.

"Look, I understand," I said, layering my voice with sugar. "But if you can manage this, I'll make sure you don't lose a single rupee from your security deposit."

There was a pause. A long one. The kind that makes you wonder if the call dropped or if the other person is calculating the square root of your soul. Finally, he agreed. Victory! Well… partial victory.

By the next day, the house was empty—almost. A few flower pots lingered on the balcony like forgotten guests at a wedding who refuse to leave even after the DJ packs up. He called me and said, "Sir, bas kuch pots reh gaye hain."

I laughed. "Manageable," I told him. "I'll talk to Gaurav. He's not buying a jungle, so a few plants won't scare him."

One problem solved. For now.

CHAPTER 20

PASSPORT PICK UP

I had promised Pandey ji that I'd meet him at Amrapali Green by afternoon, but first, there was another mission on my list—the passport pickup. My prized possession was waiting at the Netaji Subhas Marg Metro Station aka VAC center and I wasn't about to keep it waiting.

I booked a cab, and the driver, in his infinite wisdom, decided to dodge traffic by taking the "shortcut" through Delhi's alleys. Shortcut? More like a scenic tour of every pothole in the city. By the time we crawled out of the maze, I was convinced Google Maps should come with a sarcasm filter: *"Fastest route? Ha-ha, good luck!"*

Finally, I reached the Metro station, paid the driver, and crossed the road like a man on a mission. Security check at the entrance—routine stuff. The USA VAC center was tucked away on the lower ground floor, and to my surprise, it was calm. No queues, no chaos. Just me and a few bored staff scrolling their phones.

I handed over my ID (a humble xerox copy of my passport) and the acknowledgment slip from Chennai VAC. A few clicks, a few stamps, and there it was—my passport, freshly stamped, gleaming like a trophy. I checked the details twice, slid it into my sling bag, and felt that sweet rush of relief. One more box ticked and I am loving it.

CHAPTER 21

THE METRO ADVENTURE

Now came the real adventure: Reach Akshardham Metro Station for the Aadhar enrollment. I wanted to give it another try as my last trial at Ranchi failed. Two options:

1. Book a cab and reach comfortably.
2. Dive into the crowd and conquer the Delhi Metro—a dream deferred since 2014.

Back then, Rupa and I had planned a metro ride, but the moment we saw the rush at Nehru Place station, we chickened out. This time, no excuses. I was going to do it. And believe me, it felt less like commuting and more like a theme park ride.

Hop on, hop off. Red Line from Netaji Subhas to Kashmere Gate, then Yellow Line to Akshardham. The trains were frequent, the ride smooth, and the AC was a blessing. But one thing bugged me—everyone was glued to their phones. No smiles, no small talk, just scrolling zombies. I'm old-school; I like a little human interaction. But hey, maybe that's too much to ask in 2025.

First thing after getting down at Akshardham Metro Station? A bottle of nimbu paani—because hydration is hope. Then I headed to the lower ground floor where the Aadhar office was. I braced for Ranchi-style crowds, but it was… manageable. Sort of. The only catch? I had arrived at peak hour, and they were closing for lunch. Perfect timing, right?

I had no clue where to go or whom to ask. Staff looked overwhelmed, people looked lost, and even the security guard—the usual savior in such situations—was drowning in questions. Finally, someone muttered about scanning a QR code to book an appointment online.

Great idea, right? I spotted the QR code stuck on the wall like a secret treasure map and scanned it. Pulled out my sister-in-law's phone—my backup weapon—and prayed for internet. Getting a signal on the lower ground floor felt like trying to win the lifeline in *Kaun Banega Crorepati*.

After a few tense moments, the page loaded. Victory! I started filling out the form, typing in every detail like a man on a mission. And then... the final submission button refused to work. Dead. Frozen. Mocking me.

I sat on the staircase, sweating, stabbing at my phone like a guy trying to defuse a bomb in an action movie. Nothing. No luck. Frustration level? Himalayan. So, without any luck at the Aadhar office, I surrendered. Booked a cab and headed back to Arvind's house, feeling like a soldier retreating after a lost battle.

I had promised Pandey ji I'd visit him at Amrapali Green, but I'd already called him during the ride back to confess:

"It's late, Pandey ji. Mission failed. I'm not coming today."

The original plan was ambitious—drop by my society office, clear the dues, and set the stage for transferring the house to the new owner. But Delhi had other plans for me. Between QR codes that refused to cooperate and metro adventures that ate up time, the day slipped away.

As the cab rolled through the evening traffic, I stared out of the window, thinking: *If this was just the warm-up, what's next?*

CHAPTER 22

TWO DAYS TO GO: THE PAPER CHASE

11th **Evening.** Two days to go for the big day—the house transfer. My mind was juggling tasks like a circus performer. One of them: coordinating with the bank guy handling Gaurav's home loan.

The bank needed to validate original documents—sale deed, allotment letter, Nagar Nigam no-dues certificate—the works. This was news to me. Pandey ji hadn't mentioned that the originals had to be shown before final approval from the bank. If I'd known, I would've landed in Delhi earlier instead of playing metro adventurer yesterday.

After a series of back-and-forth calls, I finally asked the bank guy to come to Arvind's house in the evening. No more chasing across the city—I'd had enough of that. He arrived, checked every paper like a jeweler inspecting diamonds, and gave the nod. Disbursal would start soon.

Pandey ji was there too, updating Gaurav:

"Validation done. One more step cleared."

I leaned back, feeling a small wave of relief. One more task off the list. But the clock was ticking, and the next two days promised more drama.

Because tomorrow wasn't just about paperwork. Tomorrow was about an **experiment**—something I'd been planning quietly, something that could change the rhythm of this trip.

CHAPTER 23

TEA, TALKS, AND TWO BIRDS

It was time to introduce you to someone special—Mr. Tapan Bhaiya. Or as I fondly call him, *Bhaiya.* A man of principle, my mentor, my advisor on everything under the sun. Well, almost everything. If the topic is IT, I wouldn't bet on him—but knowing Bhaiya, he'd probably prove me wrong just to make a point. He's an electrical engineering purist, the kind who can make transformers sound poetic, and now runs his own venture like a seasoned captain steering his ship.I know him for last 21 years now.He shared the same wing where my to be sold flat is.Now he lives in a new society close to that.

I was in Delhi on my second day and still hadn't visited his place. He new house is just a few blocks away from Aravind's house. Rupa had been nudging me too: *"When are you going to meet them?"* So, I decided—enough procrastination. Today was the day.

Aravind was back from office, and little Avyaa was home too. I asked him if he'd like to tag along. Last time I was in Delhi, I had already broken the ice between him and Bhaiya, so they weren't strangers anymore. Aravind checked with Seema if Avyaa could come. He wasn't sure if she'd enjoy the company—or let us talk. But finally, she agreed to join us.

We reached Bhaiya's society, greeted by the security guards, and filled out the visitor form. Guest parking? That was another puzzle. The guard gave us a vague hint: "Park near the society temple." So we did, hoping divine blessings would protect the car.

I had picked up a box of sweets—because in India, you don't visit family empty-handed. We took the lift to Tower 3 and rang the bell. The door opened, and there was Himanshi Bhabhi, all smiles. Honestly, every time I meet her, she looks younger—and so does Bhaiya. Maybe they've cracked the anti-aging code, and it's hidden in their tea.

Bhaiya appeared after a few minutes, his trademark calm aura filling the room. We settled on the couch. I reintroduced Aravind and Avyaa. Avyaa, meanwhile, found a new friend—Tia. Tia is Tapan Bhaiya's younger daughter and practically family to me; I've known her since Day 1. Watching her grow from a toddler to an high schooler feels surreal.

Here's the twist: this wasn't just a social visit. I had invited Pandey ji and Gaurav—the buyer of my apartment—so I could kill two birds with one stone. Meet Bhaiya, and also meet Gaurav face-to-face for the first time. Until now, we'd only spoken over the phone.

Bhabhi brought snacks and tea (no sugar for me). She was already in the loop that I am avoiding sugar, thanks to her regular chats with Rupa. That saved me a lot of explaining. Bhaiya and Aravind caught up while I mentally rehearsed my pitch for Gaurav.

Soon, Bhaiya got a call from the society gate: "Sir, some visitors are here." It was Pandey ji and Gaurav. Bhaiya told the guard to let them in. I advised Pandey ji to try parking near the temple—our unofficial guest parking zone.

Finally, they arrived and joined us on the couch. My first impression of Gaurav? A typical NCR guy—practical, sharp, and straight to the point. We exchanged pleasantries, and I did a quick background check: where he works, family details, and why he wanted my apartment. Then we discussed next steps—the registry, the timeline, and the elephant in the room: the low TDS certificate. Without it, Gaurav couldn't finalize the tax deduction. With Rakhi holidays and government babuism , we weren't optimistic about meeting the 14th deadline.

I assured him the tenant had vacated, and I'd collect the keys tomorrow—12th August. That seemed to ease his mind. We had a plan. Tea (round two for me) and some crunchy makhana fry kept the conversation flowing.

Pandey ji and Gaurav left after a while. We decided to wrap up too, so Bhaiya and Bhabhi could have dinner. But Avyaa had other plans. She was having the time of her life in Tia's room—coloring, playing, and ignoring our pleas. After a mini-drama, we called Seema for backup. Only a mother's voice could break the spell. Finally, Avyaa agreed, and we headed back.

I started my office work late that night, catching up on emails like a man chasing a departing train. Don't remember what time I slept, but one thing was clear—it was an eventful day.

Tomorrow? Collecting keys, clearing dues, and maybe a miracle on that TDS certificate. The clock was ticking, and the story was far from over.

CHAPTER 24

ONE DAY TO GO AND SECOND CHANCE AT AKSHARDHAM

I woke up at the usual time, finished my morning routine, and walked into the living room. Shalini was busy getting Avyaa ready for play school. That was my cue—the moment to showcase my acting skills. Honestly, I'd been trained for this since Day 1 at Arvind's house.

Here's the deal: Avyaa loves having people around to play with. If she sees Arvind and Seema at home (they leave for office by 9 a.m.), she refuses to go to school. Convincing her is a full-blown mission.

The plan? After her bath, Shalini gets her dressed in her room. Meanwhile, the three of us—me, Arvind, and Seema—lock ourselves in the master bedroom. Avyaa is told that Mom and Dad have left for work and Uncle has gone out early for errands. With no one left to play with, she has no choice but to head to school.

Once she steps out with Shalini, that's our signal to emerge from hiding and resume our routine. Seema usually watches the whole episode on her phone, streaming from the living room camera. The moment Avyaa and Shalini cross the main door, we're free.

Today's key task: apply for my Aadhaar card. Thankfully, last night before bed, I managed to book an appointment on the Aadhaar site—11:15 a.m. sharp.

By the time I glanced at the clock, it was already 9 a.m. Panic mode activated as this is the office rush time. I have stayed at this place for solid five years and know it really well. I rushed through getting ready, grabbed a quick breakfast, and booked a cab to the Aadhaar office at Akshardham Metro Station—the same battlefield where I had tasted defeat yesterday.

The cab ride felt like a second chance. I reached the building and headed straight to the lower ground floor. It took me a moment to figure out the setup—queues and the counters. I approached the security guard managing the crowd and flashed my appointment confirmation on my phone. That little PDF felt like **Sanjeevani**—my lifeline for the day.

He nodded and pointed me to a queue leading to a counter. Hardly five people ahead of me. Soon, it was my turn. I told the man at the counter I was here for a fresh Aadhaar card. His expression? Pure bewilderment. Probably wondering what I was doing at this age without an Aadhaar card in India. Fair question.

He asked if I had all the documents. I said yes—PAN card (active now, thanks to Arvind the CA) to prove my identity, sale deed of the house (which will officially change hands tomorrow) to establish my India Adress and establishment, passport with an active visa to prove my NRI status, and photographs I had gotten done in Chennai. The sale deed was my trump card, though I didn't reveal that I was selling the house. His silence was golden—it meant everything was in order. He handed me a chit with my appointment number and asked me to step inside.

The moment I entered, a cool breeze from the AC greeted me like an old friend. The place was well-managed, with a decent waiting lobby. I knew it would take time—there were plenty of people ahead, most updating phone numbers or addresses, or enrolling their kids. Only a handful were there for fresh Aadhaar enrollment.

I settled into a chair and struck up a conversation with a young guy next to me. He had just completed his undergrad and was working for an IT company in Noida. That was refreshing—India's IT job market seemed healthy, unlike the U.S., where layoffs and AI-driven automation were squeezing opportunities. I felt genuinely happy for him. Shared a bit about what I do and why I was there.

On my other side, two boys were squeezed into one chair, each trying to push the other off. Classic sibling rivalry—still organic, still fun. I teased them a little and chatted with their dad. They were from Haryana. The kids proudly told me each of them had two cows and loved milk. That's Haryana for you—milk, cows, buffaloes, wrestling, and Audis. They spoke in Haryanvi, and suddenly, I was transported back to 2001–2002, remembering the blue-line bus conductors with Haryanvi accent and attitude during my Delhi days.

My token number—31—flashed on the screen. Showtime. I walked to the assigned desk and sat down. The desk was a classic Aadhaar setup: a monitor , a keyboard and a small webcam perched like a security guard on duty. Behind it sat the dear officer.The first step was document validation. Most people submit a utility bill for address proof. Me? I had a twenty-page sale deed. Definitely not their everyday case.

I couldn't use my apartment's utility bill because it wasn't issued by the UP government—it was just an A4 sheet from the society office. No official seal, no credibility. So, the sale deed was my best bet.

The officer initiated my application and handed me a one-page printout. Then came the twist: I had to take this page to another desk for endorsement. Counter 8. A lady was handling validations there. I waited, handed over my papers, and watched her eyebrows rise at the sight of the sale deed. Not the usual stuff.

She asked me to visit the cabin of the center's chief officer. That threw me off. My mind raced—*Will he even be there? If he is, will he entertain me or ask me to come later? Will this derail my mission?*

With those thoughts swirling, I walked to his cabin and waited outside. Through the glass, I could see him talking to a subordinate. He saw me too. For a moment, it felt like a silent staring contest After a few minutes, he called me in.

I explained my case. He took the documents, flipped through the pages, checked everything carefully, and finally wrote **"Validated"** on my application printout. Then, he signed it with the flourish of someone who knows the power of his pen. Quick. Efficient. No drama.

I thanked him and returned to the lady at Counter 8. She endorsed the page. Validation complete. Mission moving forward.

Next step: the grand finale—entering details into the system, scanning and uploading documents, and capturing biometrics.

I returned to the desk and sat next to the officer. He asked me to look into the camera. *Click.* The photo popped up on the screen. Not bad—I had lost some weight. For a moment, I thought, "Can I get a copy of this for LinkedIn?"

Then came the fingerprinting. The software was designed to show a green check for each finger if the scan was proper. Sounds simple, right? Wrong. My fingers apparently had trust issues. The officer had to press them down like he was kneading dough. After multiple trials, the system finally accepted them. Victory.

Next: document scanning and upload. Generally uploading documents is a routine task—fast servers, smooth process. Here? Welcome to the slow-motion world. The scanner groaned like an old man climbing stairs, and the upload speed made me nostalgic for dial-up internet. I even tried striking up a conversation about the issue, wearing my "Solution Architect" hat:

"Sir, maybe you could schedule uploads during off-peak hours to reduce load?"

He gave me a look that said, *'We have put a request for new scanners.'*

I said "Great".

Finally, the uploads went through. Just when I thought I was done, another twist: the officer's software version didn't have the option to submit an application as an NRI. He tried a few times, sighed, and sent me to another desk. Twenty more minutes of waiting. I killed time by overhearing staff conversations—classic office talk about being overworked and overstretched.

One scene caught my attention: an officer was helping a blind applicant. The process requires a retina scan, and obviously, that wasn't working. The supervisor—the same center head who validated my documents—stepped in and said, "Upload whatever image you can capture. Back office will handle it." Practical wisdom at its best.

Finally, my turn came. Same process again—photo reclicked, retina image captured, documents scanned and uploaded. The upload speed was still crawling. If I had admin rights, I would've restarted the machine to clear the cache. But I wasn't the boss, so all I could do was cross my fingers and pray the connection didn't drop mid-process.

The officer, though, was a man of patience. While mine was tearing apart, he calmly navigated every glitch. After 40 minutes of sitting there, all formalities were complete. He handed me the acknowledgment number and instructions to check the status online.

Two hours—including waiting and processing—and I walked out victorious. Honestly, I hadn't expected it to be done today, given my previous experiences with government offices. Hats off to Akshardham Aadhaar Center—they were doing a perfect job. Keep it up.

CHAPTER 25

THE KEYS THAT WAITED FIFTEEN YEARS

My next task was simple on paper: head straight to my renter's new house, just one block away from my own. Pandey ji was supposed to meet me there. I grabbed a cab from Akshardham Metro Station and reached the marketing complex in front of my society. No sign of Pandey ji.

I called him.

"Bas aa raha hoon… thoda time lagega," he said in his trademark calm tone.

Translation: *I'm on my way, but don't hold your breath.*

Pandey ji and punctuality have a long-distance relationship. If he says "five minutes," you can easily finish a cup of tea, scroll Facebook, and maybe even write a short poem before he arrives. I told him I'd use the time wisely and collect the house keys from my renter.

My renter, Subhashis Mishra, had rented the house for years. I called him; he was at the office but said his wife was home and I could pick up the keys from her. Perfect.

I knew this community well. Back in our Indirapuram days, this marketing complex was our go-to spot for South Indian snacks. There was a family-owned tiffin center that served idlis and dosas that could make Chennai proud. I still remember those evenings—me, Rupa, and baby Aarna sitting at a steel table, sambhar aroma filling the air, and the owner shouting, "Extra chutney, sir?" That place was our comfort zone in a city that never slowed down.

I got the flat number, made the entry at the gate, and rang the doorbell. His wife—whom I had met before—opened the door. Subhashis had already given her a heads-up. She asked me to sit, offered water, and handed me the house keys. The keys felt heavy—not in weight, but in memories. After fifteen years, they were back in my hand. The house had been rented since 2010—the year I switched jobs, joined Accenture Hyderabad, and later moved to Bangalore. Life had moved fast; the keys hadn't.

She offered snacks, but I politely declined. Two reasons: I was avoiding sweets and snacks, and Pandey ji was waiting… or at least, theoretically waiting. I thanked her, stepped out, and walked towards my society Amrapali Green's Entrance gate next block. Finally, I spotted Pandey ji standing near the entrance, looking like a man who had just finished a marathon. We exchanged greetings and headed toward the entry gate together.

As we walked, a wave of anxiety hit me. Fifteen years. I was about to step into a house that had been someone else's home for so long. I wasn't expecting it to be in great condition—how could I? But still, my mind raced: *Will it feel like mine? Or just a stranger's space with my name on the papers?* The keys in my hand suddenly felt heavier than ever.

CHAPTER 26

THE HOUSE THAT TIME FORGOT

Pandey ji was the official property agent of this society, so getting past the security guards was a breeze. No questions asked—his reputation was the passcode. Since I had the key, I suggested, "Let's see the house first." He nodded, and I handed him the key to open the iron gate and then the main door.

The moment the door creaked open, reality hit me like a bucket of cold water. The house was in a mess. One reason: the renter hadn't bothered to clean up after moving out. But honestly, most of the damage had been done during their stay. Electric switches were hanging like loose teeth, bathroom mirrors had lost their silver coating, and the kitchen utility room looked like a dump yard.

Then came the real shocker—garbage piled against the living room wall: dust, paper scraps, and hair. That was the area hidden behind their furniture all these years. I stood there thinking aloud, *How can someone live like this?* The house was in decent shape when I visited in 2022. What happened? Maybe the classic renter mindset: *We're leaving anyway, so why care?*

Pandey ji shared the same thoughts, shaking his head like a disappointed school principal. I didn't make it an issue because Gaurav, the new buyer, had plans to remodel the house completely. Most fittings would change, and the place would get a fresh makeover. He wasn't bothered about the wear and tear—or the mess. Since he didn't fuss, I stayed silent. Otherwise, I would have happily deducted every rupee from Subhashis's security deposit. Instead, I asked Subhashis to come tomorrow evening to collect his deposit.

Pandey ji, meanwhile, had other ideas brewing.

"Sir," he said, pointing at the ceiling fans, "Are these yours?"

"Yes," I replied.

He grinned. "Anyway, the new owner will remodel everything. He'll throw out the fans, RO machine, exhaust system… Why waste? Can I take the fans?"

I laughed. "Go ahead. Better to use them than trash them."

There was also a lonely chair and table left behind. I told Pandey ji to take them for his office. After staying there for a few minutes, we locked the main gate. I kept the key—it would go to the new owner tomorrow if all ducks lined up.

Initially, I had planned to do a WhatsApp video call with Rupa and show her the house one last time—the house she had once chosen for us. But looking at the mess, I changed my mind. Instead, I clicked a couple of pictures for memory and moved on.

Our next stop: the society maintenance office in the lower basement. The maintenance office was tucked away in the lower basement—a place that smelled faintly of damp concrete and old files. The corridor leading to it had peeling paint and a notice board cluttered with faded circulars about water supply timings and "No Parking" warnings.

Pandey ji walked in like a man who owned the place. He was a regular here, and his confidence was the passcode. The maintenance supervisor greeted him with a nod that said, *"Here comes trouble, but the good kind."*

Pandey ji introduced me, and I explained the purpose: selling the house and clearing all dues. The supervisor pulled out a thick ledger book—the kind that makes you wonder if computers were just a rumor here. My renter had already cleared maintenance till August 15, and I got the receipt for that.

Then came the big one: the 0.5% of the total sale value payable to the RWA for the no-dues certificate. I had planned for this. Gaurav's token money was sitting in my Indian account, and I was carrying my sister-in-law's phone from Ranchi for UPI payments. I quickly scanned the QR code on PhonePe and made the payment. The beep of successful transaction felt like music in that basement silence.

The supervisor handed me the no-dues certificate—a single sheet of paper that held the power to unlock tomorrow's deal. I slid it carefully into my sling bag like it was a winning lottery ticket.

I thanked Pandey ji, who was already chatting with the staff about cricket scores and property gossip. Before leaving, I told him, "Let's sync in the evening and plan for tomorrow." He nodded, and we walked out of the basement, leaving behind the hum of AC and my nostalgia.

CHAPTER 27

THE CERTIFICATE THAT SAVED THE DAY

Just when I thought all ducks were in a row, one stubborn duck decided to swim away. The roadblock? Gaurav's home loan. The bank would only disburse the amount once he paid his contribution—including TDS. And to pay TDS, Gaurav needed the **low TDS certificate**, which my CA, Arvind, had applied for after my PAN card became active.

The problem? The TDS application was still in progress. When I checked with Arvind CA at 10 a.m. in the morning on the way to Aadhar office , he said, "Next update in the afternoon." That was not comforting. If I didn't get the certificate by evening, Gaurav couldn't pay TDS to the Income Tax Department. No TDS, no loan disbursement. And without that, tomorrow's registration would collapse like a house of cards. My travel plan back to the U.S.? Jeopardized.

I started contemplating backup plans. With these thoughts swirling, I booked an auto on Rapido and headed to Arvind's house. Shalini and Avyaa were taking a nap. Shalini opened the door, and I told her, "Serve me lunch and continue your nap." I freshened up, had lunch, and opened my laptop to check the damage: how much extra would it cost to delay my flight by a week?

I logged into Qatar Airways. The number stared back at me—$350 extra. Painful, but manageable if needed. Next, I had to inform my manager and seek permission for an extended stay. For that, I had to wait till 7 p.m. (U.S. working hours).

Arvind returned from office around 6 p.m. I updated him on the day's developments and the urgency of the TDS certificate. I told him I had called Arvind—the CA—in the afternoon. He was in his hometown in UP. If the certificate wasn't issued tonight, he promised to get it done tomorrow morning after his early flight back to Delhi. I also shared my backup plan: checked ticket prices, calculated the extra cost, and mentally prepared for a delay if my manager approved.

Arvind listened quietly as I laid out the situation—the TDS certificate, the ticking clock, the looming risk of delaying the registration and my flight. When I finished, he leaned back, gave me that trademark half-smile, and said,

"Call the CA. Give me the phone."

That was it. No panic, no drama—just pure confidence. Arvind was in his element now. He slipped into his client-relationship mode like a seasoned negotiator walking into a boardroom. His voice was calm but carried weight:

"Boss, aaj hi karna hai. Jugaad lagao. Registry kal honi chahiye."

It wasn't a request; it was a directive. The kind that makes people move mountains—or at least push a few files faster. He didn't reveal my backup plan, didn't show any cards. Just pressure, delivered with charm.

The CA promised to try his best. By 8 p.m., my phone buzzed. The CA said, "Certificate approved. Sending screenshots." I stared at the screen like it was a lottery win. For the first time, I saw the TDS certificate – a document with a reference code Gaurav needed for online payment.

Finally, all ducks were back in the row. I called Pandey ji and gave him the good news. "Update Gaurav and ask him to pay the TDS online using the details on the certificate," I said.

"Yes, sir," he replied, sounding relieved. Then added, "One of my guys will pick you up tomorrow morning from Arvind's society."

"Perfect," I said, exhaling for what felt like the first time all day.

Meanwhile, I was ready to throw a party for a PDF file.

CHAPTER 28

THE MARATHON BEFORE THE FINISH LINE

Today felt like a marathon with checkpoints scattered across Delhi. It started at **Akshardham Aadhaar Center**, where I fought the battle—fingerprints, slow uploads, and the final victory of getting my acknowledgment slip. From there, it was a quick cab ride to the society, collecting the **keys after fifteen years**, only to find the house left in a state that could make a horror movie set designer proud. Dust, broken switches, and a kitchen that looked like a dump yard.

Then came the maintenance office visit in the basement—a world of ledgers, QR codes, and air conditioner that hummed louder than they cooled. I walked out with the **no-dues certificate**, feeling like I had unlocked Level 2 of this property game.

But the real tension was brewing in the background—the **TDS certificate**. Without it, tomorrow's registration would collapse, and my flight back to the U.S. would turn into a $350 headache. I even checked Qatar Airways for backup plans, mentally preparing for a delay.

And then, just when the day was about to end in uncertainty, Arvind stepped in like a Bollywood hero. One phone call, a dose of *jugaad*, and by 8 p.m., the CA sent me the screenshot: **TDS certificate approved**. That single PDF felt like a golden ticket.

As I put my phone down, a sense of calm washed over me. All ducks were finally in a row. Pandey ji confirmed the pickup for tomorrow morning. The stage was set.

Tomorrow is the **D-Day**—the day this house officially stops being mine. A house that once held dreams, laughter, and countless cups of chai. Tonight, I'm not thinking about the mess or the money. I'm thinking about closure. And maybe, just maybe, a quiet goodbye.

CHAPTER 29

THE D-DAY – FROM DRIZZLE TO GOODBYE

I woke up excited. All the prerequisites were done. Today was the final act—the day this house would officially stop being mine. After my morning routine, I called Pandey ji to check when his guy would pick me up. Outside, the weather was playing its part perfectly—soft drizzle, a gray sky, and that earthy smell of wet soil. It felt like nature was scripting a cinematic farewell.

A few minutes later, my phone buzzed with an unknown number. It was Pandey ji's guy. I grabbed my sling bag, checked the original sale deed and other mandatory documents, and headed to the society gate, dodging raindrops like a reluctant dancer. He was waiting in a white Swift. I confirmed the ride and slid in. Time: 9:30 a.m.

We drove to Pandey ji's office, barely a kilometer away. Pandey ji was already waiting on the roadside, umbrella in hand, looking like a man who had seen too many property deals to be fazed by drizzle. He hopped in. I asked if Gaurav and his wife had left; Pandey ji nodded. I double-checked with him about the documents needed for registration. His calm "Yes, sir" was reassuring.

The drizzle continued as we started for the Ghaziabad Registry Office—the same place where I had registered this house back in 2006. A full circle moment. Pandey ji wasn't your typical property agent—no unnecessary chatter, no big talk. But the driver? He was the opposite. A young hustler managing PG accommodations for students and working women in Indirapuram. His phone buzzed every few minutes—clients calling about issues, prospects asking for vacancies. I was impressed. This guy was building an empire one phone call at a time.

Traffic was light until we neared the Registry Office. Then came the chaos—puddles, cars honking, and people hopping like frogs to avoid waterlogged patches. We found a pay-and-park spot after some maneuvering. Gaurav and his wife, Mukta, had also arrived. I met Mukta for the first time—warm smile despite the weather. Pandey ji led the way, and we followed, balancing on footpaths and playing "jumping jack" over puddles.

Finally, we reached our lawyer's chamber—a two-floor setup. The ground floor was buzzing with daily visitors, so we were ushered upstairs. The first floor was a relief—air-conditioned and quiet. I handed over my ID proof, passport-size photo, and signed a few documents. Gaurav and Mukta did the same. Things were moving smoothly. Tea was offered. I initially declined—sugar-free wasn't an option—but later gave in. The tea was good, and the best part? We didn't have to move an inch for it. Outside, the drizzle continued, adding a calm backdrop to the day.

Now came the wait for the bank guy—the man with the cheque. This was the amount Gaurav and Mukta had borrowed to complete the payment. Rule of registration: full payment before signing. Gaurav had already transferred a portion online; the bank was financing the rest. Pandey ji called to check his ETA. Finally, he arrived—the most important person in the room now. He began validating documents like a cashier checking currency notes. Sale deed, builder-buyer agreement, possession letter—all dated 2006 but in pristine condition. One round of validation had already happened on Monday, but today, he was the boss.

Then came the twist. A discrepancy in Mukta's surname. Minor, but enough for him to make a fuss. We tried convincing him, but he wasn't budging. He knew his power. Finally, Pandey ji and Gaurav escalated to his supervisor, explaining the urgency. A quick call later, approval came through. Another roadblock cleared.

Most formalities were handled in the lawyer's office—signatures, thumb impressions, and document checks. The finish line was in sight.

The lawyer slid the new sale deed across the table like a dealer in a high-stakes poker game. I picked up the pen, and for a second, my hand hesitated. Fifteen years of memories flashed—our first Diwali in that house, the laughter echoing in the living room, the smell of chole from the kitchen on lazy Sundays. And now, all of it was about to become history with one signature.

I signed. My name flowed across the page, steady but heavy. Gaurav and Mukta followed suit, their faces glowing with excitement. For them, this was the start of a dream. For me, it was closure. Thumb impressions came next—pressing my fingers into the ink pad felt oddly symbolic, like leaving fingerprints on a chapter I was closing forever.

Pandey ji, ever the professional, checked every page like a schoolteacher reviewing homework. "Sir, ek aur sign yahan," he said, pointing at a corner I had missed. I joked, "Pandey ji, by the end of this, I'll forget my own signature." He chuckled softly—the kind of laugh that says, *I've heard this a hundred times today.*

Finally, the lawyer declared, "Ho gaya." Done. Just like that.

Then came the **handover of keys**—the moment I had been dreading and anticipating in equal measure. I reached into my sling bag and pulled out the keys that had been mine for nineteen years. They felt heavier than yesterday, not because of metal, but because of memories. I handed them to Gaurav with a smile that tried to hide the lump in my throat.

"Take care of the house," I said.

He nodded, "Definitely, sir." Mukta added, "We'll make it beautiful."

I believed her. And that made it easier.

Pandey ji, sensing the emotional weight, broke the silence with his trademark practicality:

"Sir, ab chai ho jaye?"

I laughed. "Pandey ji, chai toh banti hai."

We sipped tea while the drizzle outside turned into a steady rain, washing the streets clean—just like today washed away a chapter of my life.

CHAPTER 30

THE LAST SIGNATURE

Now came the final leg: both parties had to go to the registrar's office in another building. We followed Pandey ji and a guy from the lawyer's office through the drizzle. The complex had that typical government vibe—crowded corridors, peeling paint, and people either genuinely busy or pretending to be.

Just as we entered, a beggar intercepted us. He looked straight at us and said,

"Lakhon lakhon ki deal karne aate hain, par ek 10 rupaye dene mein inki phat ti hai."

Translation: *You come here for deals worth lakhs, but hesitate to give ten rupees.*

I wasn't in the mood for guilt trips, so I ignored him and walked on with the group. Pandey ji didn't flinch either—he's seen it all.

Inside, the registrar's office was buzzing with activity. Pandey ji, being a regular, navigated the maze like a pro. Thanks to him, our formalities were wrapped up in about 30 minutes. While waiting, I got talking with Gaurav and Mukta. Gaurav was the quiet type, but Mukta? She was like me—loved to talk. She asked about my family, and I asked about hers. She told me about their daughter and their pet. The ice melted quickly, and suddenly, this didn't feel like a transaction—it felt human.

Then came the moment. I congratulated both of them. At that exact time, the bank guy handed the cheque to Gaurav, and Gaurav officially passed it to me. **100% payment done.** For a second, it felt surreal—like a dream. But it was real, in broad daylight.

Pandey ji pulled us aside for the final checklist:

"Maintenance paid till 15th, utilities cleared, bills settled."

He was thorough, making sure my chapter closed cleanly and theirs started fresh. I was genuinely impressed by his professionalism. He promised to send me a copy of the new sale deed for my records.

Gaurav gave some money to buy sweets for the lawyer's assistant—a small gesture that felt like tradition. We had tea one last time. I shook Gaurav's hand, firm and warm, and wished him and his family a pleasant, fruitful stay in the house that had been mine for fifteen years.

Before he got into his car, I told him, "I'll share the login details for utilities—IGL, LPG pipeline—so you can transfer them to your name." He nodded gratefully.

And just like that, it was done. The big change: **Gaurav is now the owner of my house.**

We three—Pandey ji, his guy, and I—got into our car and started back toward Indirapuram. The drizzle had turned into a steady rain, washing the streets clean. It felt symbolic—like the day had washed away a chapter of my life.

What a sigh of relief. Everything that seemed impossible and undoable at one point was finally done. The registry—**Project D-Day**—was successful.

For the last fifteen days, my mind had been in constant motion—thinking, executing, coordinating. From landing in Chennai to reaching

Indirapuram, every step felt like a mini-project. And now, the biggest milestone was behind me. The mental churn finally slowed down.

All the plans were falling into place. But wait—there's another chapter in this story. Just when I thought the curtain had fallen, a new name entered the script: **Prestige Indirapuram**.

CHAPTER 31

THE UPGRADE - ASHIYANA 2.0

Another important task after selling the house was deciding what to do with the proceeds. For us, the answer was clear: reinvest in another property. Thankfully, back in July—while we were still contemplating selling our existing house—we had already figured out the next move: book a **3 BHK in Prestige Indirapuram.Lifestyle has upgraded in the last 20 years—from a humble 2 BHK to a proud 3 BHK.**

Now, let me be honest—it was way above our original budget. But sometimes, you take a leap of faith. The plan was smart: the booking was under a **construction-linked payment plan**, giving us four years to make the full payment. If things changed along the way, we could always sell the unit after the two-year lock-in period. For now, the immediate requirement was 10 % of the amount for booking —and most of that came from this sale. So, the strategy was in place, and the deal was executed.

One house gone, but the replacement plan was ready. We still had our **ashiyana in Indirapuram, NCR**. Will we ever live there? I say yes—after I retire (early or traditional). Either I'll stay in India permanently or keep visiting often. And by then, age and health will limit mobility, so I wanted a place where everything is within reach—amenities, security, convenience. Prestige ticked all the boxes. Perfect timing, perfect plan.

From a financial perspective, this was also a smart move—helpful for income tax planning. And beyond numbers, this house will be more than bricks and walls. It will be a **guest house for friends**—a place where the keys will always be ready when someone visits Delhi.

The initial payment was made, and the **builder-buyer agreement signed**. I even managed to visit the site and was impressed—the location, the sample flats, the vibe. It felt like the right decision. A new chapter was beginning, even as the old one closed.

CHAPTER 32

FROM SELLER TO INVESTOR IN 30 MINUTES

Coming back to the original thread—me, Pandey ji, and his accomplice drove back to Indirapuram. The drive was surprisingly pleasant. The drizzle continued, painting the roads in a glossy sheen, and traffic was light. For the first time in days, I felt a little calm.

I asked Pandey ji to drop me at **HDFC Bank**. The plan was simple: deposit the cheque. The clock, however, was not on my side. It was **2:20 p.m.**, and the bank was supposed to close for public transactions by **2:30 p.m.** Ten minutes. I wasn't sure if they'd accept the cheque this late, but I had to try.

I rushed inside, found the teller, and explained my situation. "Can I still deposit this cheque? I have to travel tomorrow," I said, hoping my urgency would help.

To be honest, that was only half the truth. I hadn't booked my tickets to Ranchi yet. Neither had I changed my return flight to the U.S. My original flight was scheduled for **17th at 4:30 a.m.**, which meant I had to be at Delhi airport on the night of the 16th. Today was already the 14th.

Reality hit me hard—I had only this afternoon to wrap up everything in Indirapuram. And deep down, I knew the plan to fly on the 17th was dead. I had barely spent time with my parents, and I was hoping to celebrate my birthday on the 16th with them before leaving. That plan now seemed like a distant dream unless I pushed my travel dates further.

As I stood there, waiting for the teller's nod, my mind was juggling scenarios—extra charges for rescheduling, manager approval for extended stay, and the ticking clock of unfinished tasks. Life felt like a chessboard, and I was playing speed chess with fate.

Back to the bank. The teller checked my account, and his eyebrows lifted slightly—it had a healthy balance now. Most of the proceeds had come from Gaurav's transfers. He had only applied for a partial loan; the rest came from his and Mukta's savings.

The teller, a fellow Bihari, quickly switched from cashier mode to investment advisor mode. He saw me as a potential client for some HDFC plan. "Sir, don't worry. I'll take care of your needs," he said with the confidence of someone selling dreams. Before I knew it, he had introduced me to his colleague—a relationship manager.

Investment wasn't mandatory, but the royal treatment I was getting made me say yes to a **multi-year investment plan**. Suddenly, I was filling multiple forms like a student sitting for an exam he didn't prepare for. PAN here, passport there, signatures everywhere. At one point, I joked, "Are we buying property again or applying for citizenship?" The manager laughed, but kept sliding more forms my way.

Thankfully, I had my passport and passport-size photos handy—because in India, these two things are like oxygen for paperwork. Meanwhile, the cheque deposit was done. The investment forms were signed and approved in the system. Money was deducted from my account. Everything was happening at lightning speed because I had what felt like a **herd of bank staff** helping me.

Finally, I met the NRI relationship manager to convert my savings account into an **NRE account**. More attention, more smiles. Money is power—proved again. Last but not least, I updated my phone number and India address. All taken care of.

I thanked the staff and stepped out of the bank, feeling like I had just finished a corporate merger. In between all this, I had called Pandey ji and asked him to wait outside. I withdrew cash from the bank and handed over his commission.

Here's what impressed me again about Pandey ji: generally, people ask for "chai-paani" or some extra for sweets—it's common. I was expecting that. To my surprise, he didn't extend the conversation. He quietly kept the money in his pocket. Professional to the core. I thanked him again and promised to stay in touch.

CHAPTER 33

ZERO DOLLARS, SIX EXTRA DAYS

I came back home, excited to narrate the day's proceedings to Arvind—but he was still at the office. I had my lunch, which was **super, super late**, and then crashed for a quick power nap. My brain needed a reboot after the marathon of signatures and chai.

First thing after waking up, I opened my laptop and updated the **spreadsheet** where I was tracking every payment from Gaurav. It wasn't just numbers—it was my way of keeping sanity in this whirlwind. I also updated the milestones and tasks. One more tick mark on the list: *Registry—Done.*

Next mission: **Qatar Airways website**. Time to figure out my return plan. I tried every possible combination—weekend departures, weekday departures—like a gamer looking for cheat codes to save money. The best deal I found was paying **$350 extra** for four additional days in India. Not bad, considering I was expecting a bigger hit.

But then came the jackpot: an option to leave on **August 22**. And guess what? **Zero dollars extra.** I stared at the screen like I had just unlocked a secret level. Six extra days in India without paying a dime? That's what I call a **win-win situation**. Without wasting a second, I confirmed the booking.

With that sorted, I booked my flight to **Ranchi for tomorrow**. All set to celebrate my birthday on the 16th with friends and family—the way I had originally dreamed. I called my brother in Ranchi and updated him about the change in plans. His reaction? Pure excitement. Mine? Relief mixed with a big smile.

CHAPTER 34

PARTY TIME

Arvind was home by 7 p.m. Shalini made tea and served both of us. I couldn't wait—I narrated the entire episode from the Registry office.

He congratulated me warmly. I thanked him for all the help he had extended in this mega project.

Arvind chuckled, "How on earth did you pull this off with so many roadblocks? No Aadhaar, no Voter ID card,no active PAN, no proper address proof… basically, nothing!"

He was pulling my leg, and honestly, he wasn't wrong. So many open threads, yet here we were.

That's when the title of this book popped into my head—**'Incomplete NRI.'** Apt, isn't it? Everything was in flux, full of dependencies and challenges.

I told him, "One thing I know—whatever I do, I put my heart into it. And eventually, God comes to my rescue. This time was no different."

Now it was time to celebrate.

I told Shalini, "No dinner at home tonight. We're going out!" My plan was to call Tapan bhaiya and his family too.

But Seema came late that day, and by the time she changed, it was almost 8:30 p.m. Luckily, the next day was a holiday—15th August. Perfect evening for an outside dinner.

Tapan bhaiya had some engagement, and Arvind was still recovering from his stomach bug. So, we decided to order food at home instead.

I said to Arvind, "Let's celebrate the milestone. How about some beer?"

We stepped out and picked up a few bottles. I still remember—it was **Bira.**

We came back with the beers. The food had already arrived, and now it was time to enjoy.

Arvind wasn't in the mood to drink—still on antibiotics—but seeing my happy face, he caved in and opened one can.

One after another, we finished six cans between us. I don't know why, but those beers did the trick. Suddenly, I had an appetite like never before. I polished off a full plate of chilli chicken—Arvind barely touched his.

He compensated by making some amazing peanuts and masala papad. Crunchy, spicy, perfect.

The setting couldn't have been better: his balcony on the 8th floor, the cool breeze brushing against us, the city lights twinkling below. Perfect company, snacks, and that sweet sense of accomplishment.

Beautiful. Satisfying.

The mood was light, and my body felt relaxed. We talked about everything under the sun. I was doing most of the talking at first, but as the evening melted into night, Arvind warmed up and became more vocal.

One conversation stood out.

I spoke about Shalini—the caretaker of Avyaa. "I wish we could get someone like her for my in-laws," I said. "They stay alone in Chas, and it keeps us worried all the time. They love that house, but we're constantly stressed about their well-being."

So, I called my brother-in-law, Ajay. He lives in Ranchi and runs a coaching center. Being local to Chas and Bokaro, he was the right person to help.

I told him my plan: "I'll come to Ranchi tomorrow, the 15th. Celebrate my birthday on the 16th. And on the 17th, we'll find a helper. Project Helper is on the horizon now."

Ajay replied, "OK bhaiya, I know one person who might be interested."

"Perfect," I said. "Let's book a cab for the whole day on the 17th and get this done."

I disconnected the call feeling hopeful.

Me and Arvind continued our chatter. It was still a nice evening. We finished dinner and then binge-watched a few episodes of the web series *Saare Jahan Se Achha*—a gripping spy story about RAW.

By the time we slept, it was 1:30 a.m. Already 15th August.

That night wasn't about fancy restaurants ,big crowds, beer or food. It was about quiet laughter, shared stories, and the feeling of crossing a big hurdle together. Sometimes, that's all you need. It was about plans taking shape, friendships deepening, and the quiet thrill of knowing tomorrow held something new.

CHAPTER 35

15TH AUGUST, MY FREEDOM DAY

My flight was at noon, so I started from Arvind's place around 9 a.m.

The roads were empty—schools and offices closed for Independence Day. It was a rare sight in Delhi. No honking, no chaos. Just calm.

A light drizzle added to the serenity. The air felt fresh, almost celebratory. Passing India Gate and Humayun's Tomb, I couldn't help but notice how different the city looked that day. You could blow your lungs out and feel pure oxygen.

It was a different world.

I reached the airport in a jiffy. Got down from the cab and made the payment using PhonePe. The app chimed,

"Aapke grahak se XYZ amount prapt hue."

That little *toong* sound? I loved it.

I thanked the cab driver and walked toward the entrance.

Now, here's something you don't expect if you've lived abroad: people queuing outside the airport for identity validation. No unauthorized entry—strict checks.

My turn came. I pulled out my passport and the soft copy of the ticket on my phone. The security guy nodded, and I was in.

Since I was only carrying a cabin bag, check-in was quick. I asked for a window seat and, luckily, got it.

Just then, my phone buzzed. A cousin called to tell me his son—my nephew—works at Delhi Airport in customs. He shared his number, and I dialed.

We'd spoken before but never met. He picked up and said,

"Uncle, I'm on the night shift today."

I laughed, "No problem. We'll meet on the 22nd when I'm back for my flight to the U.S."

We hung up.

Boarding was smooth. I settled into my window seat, and as the plane taxied, I looked out at the wet tarmac glistening under the monsoon sky.

The engines roared, and soon we were airborne. Delhi shrank beneath me—its monuments, its chaos, its calm—all fading into a patchwork of green and grey.

Above the clouds, the world felt different. The sun peeked through like a shy guest. I pressed my forehead against the glass, watching the silver wings slice through the sky.

It was Independence Day, and somehow, being up here felt symbolic—free, unbound, soaring.

My thoughts drifted to Ranchi. For me, Ranchi isn't just a city. It's a pause button. A place where life slows down, where conversations aren't rushed, and where the air smells of earth after rain.

Tomorrow was my birthday, and the day after, Project Helper would begin. But for now, I just wanted to savor this moment—the calm above the clouds, the promise of home, and the quiet pride of being in a country that still celebrates freedom with such heart.

Ranchi welcomed me with more drizzle and pleasant weather. My brother and Akshu came to pick me up from the airport.

We reached home and I shared the whole Delhi episode or rather mini web series with my mom and brother. After dinner, I just called it a day.

That night, as I lay in bed listening to the rain, I felt a strange mix of gratitude and anticipation. Life was moving—sometimes slowly, sometimes in leaps—but always forward.

Tomorrow would be special.

CHAPTER 36

16TH AUGUST – MY BIRTHDAY IN RANCHI

I woke up to the sweetest surprise—both Gungun and Akshu tiptoed into my room early in the morning and shouted,

"Happy Birthday, Jetha baba!"

They had to rush for school, so their wishes were quick but heartfelt. That's the kind of start you want on your birthday.

I got ready and finished the puja. Basically, I thanked the Almighty for all the kindness he has showered on me and prayed for the same grace for the rest of my life. Then came the blessings from Mom and Dad—the kind that makes you feel grounded no matter where you live.

Lunch was a treat. Mom and Ruma had cooked all my favorites. If Mom had her way, she would have made masoor dal pakoda too. But since I was controlling my diet, she kept it simple—still, the **begun bhaja**, fluffy omelette, and **pyaz-postu** were there.

Every bite tasted like childhood.

Meanwhile, my phone was buzzing non-stop—WhatsApp messages, calls, and in-person wishes. I felt blessed. Honestly, that's the real treasure—having so many loving and caring people around you.

The afternoon was quiet. Just me soaking in the warmth of home.

Evening was for the big plan—birthday dinner. The toss-up was between two restaurants: one close to home and another far but worth the miles. We settled for the distant one—**Kavs**, the sister branch of the legendary **Kaveri**.

Kaveri is a Ranchi icon. My memories go back to the '80s and '90s when going there was a once-a-year luxury during Durga Puja. Their **mix veg** and **malai kofta** were pure magic.

Just then, my local friend Bhupesh Chaudhary called to wish me. When I told him about the dinner plan, he said,

"Great choice! I know the manager there. I'll book a table for you."

Only in India can you have two references for the same restaurant. My brother also knew the manager because of his food license consultancy side hustle.

So, the dinner gang was my brother Titu, Akshu, and Gungun. Dad preferred to stay home. I also invited Ajay (Nishu's husband) and Shinu bhaiya's family. Shinu bhaiya's son, Shakti, shares my birthday—so I had to pick a gift for him.

On the way, near Sujata Cinema, I asked Titu to stop the car. I dashed into Reliance Mart, grabbed two T-shirts—one for Shakti and one for Atharva (Nishu's son). The billing queue was long, and I was in a hurry. So, I politely requested the cashier,

"Bhaiya, just two items. I'm getting late. Can you help?"

He smiled and obliged. I rushed back to the car like a man on a mission.

Soon, Ajay and Shinu bhaiya arrived with gifts for me. I handed over Shakti's gift. Shinu Bhaiya was also joined by his wife and Ajay came with his son, Atarva. The kids—Akshu, Shakti, and Gungun and Atharva —took charge of the order. I gave them full freedom.

Not sure after how many years I was celebrating my birthday in Ranchi. The kids did justice to the menu—soups, starters, mains, desserts. I only insisted on one thing:

"Order the Hot and Sour soup. It's a must!"

The food was delicious. The company even better. We laughed, clicked pictures, and soaked in the moment.

When the bill came, it was around ₹4,000—and then a 10% discount. Three families, one of Ranchi's best restaurants, and such a modest bill. Absolutely no complaints.

As we stepped out, the gatekeeper gave us a traditional salute. I couldn't resist—I handed him ₹500 and clicked a picture with him. Only in India do you get this royal treatment.

And of course, no dinner is complete without paan. Ajay arranged them, and with that, the evening wrapped up beautifully.

On the way home, I felt a quiet joy. Great food, great company, and a day full of blessings. While having dinner, I also discussed tomorrow's plan with Ajay—the start of **Project Helper**.

Tomorrow, the real work begins.

CHAPTER 37

17TH AUGUST – PROJECT HELPER ADVENTURE

I woke up fresh, ready for the mission. The plan was clear: Ajay would pick me up with the driver, and we'd head to Asonmoni (a small village 150 kilometers from Ranchi on Bokaro to Dhanbad highway) to meet the prospective helper.

I called Ajay to check,

"When will you reach?"

He replied,

"By 9:30, Bhaiya. It's Sunday, so coaching is closed. Today, you're my student!"

I laughed, "Student, yes—but the syllabus is a bit different."

The helper we were going to meet was known to Ajay's ex-cook. So first stop: the cook's village—Asonmoni.

It was 8 a.m., so I had an hour and a half to get ready. I glanced through the newspaper. The headlines were still dominated by the sad demise of **Shibu Soren**, the tribal guru and the flagbearer for Jharkhand's statehood movement.

He was called **Dishom Guru** by the Santhal community—"Guru of the Nation." The roads for the past few days had been leading to his native near Ramgarh and Gola, as political bigwigs paid their respects.

Reading that, I felt a pang of nostalgia and pride. This land has seen struggles, sacrifices, and dreams fulfilled. Today, I was on a small mission of my own—but it felt connected somehow.

By 9:30, Ajay arrived in a white Swift Dzire, honking lightly. I stepped out, and he greeted me with his trademark grin.

"Let's go, Bhaiya. Adventure begins now!"

My mom offered him breakfast, but he politely declined and settled for a cup of tea.

The weather was perfect for a long drive—clouds hanging low, a gentle breeze, and that earthy smell after rain. The plan was clear: head to his village, about 150 km from Ranchi and roughly 25 km from my in-laws' place in Chas. First, visit the village, then stop at Chas for lunch before returning home.

We started around 10 a.m. Ajay told the driver,

"Be prepared for a late return. It's going to be a full-day trip."

The driver nodded, probably calculating how many cups of tea he'd need to survive the day.

It was monsoon season, and **Indra Dev** had been generous this year. Every pond, reservoir, and drain was brimming with water. As far as the eye could see—miles and miles of lush greenery.

The driver took the inner road via **Getalsud Dam**, then Ormanjhi, and onward to Sikidiri. This stretch is where the **Chotanagpur Ghats** begin—the land of Jharkhand's famous waterfalls like Hundru and Jonha.

The roads here are carved out of rock, spiraling up the hills and then winding down in graceful curves. I've traveled these ghats since childhood. Back then, "vacation" meant visiting my grandparents in

Bokaro, in a village called Chandipur, about 10 km off the highway. The last leg was always on a bullock cart.

Those memories came rushing back as we climbed higher.

The **Sikidiri Ghati road** is a masterpiece—hairpin bends, dramatic turns, and panoramic views of emerald hills. A canal snakes through the valley, feeding a power plant, and a small waterfall glistens nearby. There's even a makeshift shrine with a faded board in Hindi.

Photographers love this stretch—and today, the photographer in me woke up.

"Let's stop here," I told Ajay.

We stepped out. The air was crisp, the hills draped in green, and the silence broken only by chirping birds and the distant hum of water. I clicked pictures like a tourist on steroids.

Nearby, a tiny shack sold tea and snacks. I joked with the shopkeeper,

"You should put up a sign in English—'Vista Point at the Ghats.' Double your sales instantly!"

He laughed, probably wondering what planet I came from.

We ordered two steaming cups of tea. No sugar-free options here, so I didn't even ask. The driver, a tea teetotaler, just smiled and waited patiently.

After tea, a quick nature call, and a few more photos, we hit the road again.

From here, we drove straight until we left the highway for a narrow **kucha road** leading to Asonmoni. Ajay had a rough idea of the route, but this was his first time on this side of the highway. He owns a dairy farm nearby, but that's on the opposite stretch.

So, we navigated the old-fashioned way—asking anyone and everyone coming from the other side. I loved it. It reminded me of summer vacations when we'd visit my grandparents. Ponds lined the road, ducks gliding on water, kids splashing and laughing. Pure nostalgia.

Finally, we stopped at a small market—a **More**, as locals call it. One tiny hotel selling a handful of items, a paan shop, and plenty of open space for, well, nature calls.

Ajay stayed on the phone with the cook, getting directions. After a few minutes, we were back in the car. Another 10–15 minutes of bumpy village roads, and we reached his house.

It was a typical single-story home with cattle roaming in the courtyard. The cook welcomed us warmly and led us inside. Ajay and I sat on two wooden chairs.

He introduced his family—two daughters, both studying. One in middle school, the other pursuing a diploma in hotel management.

I smiled. **This is the new India—where even in remote villages, education is a priority.**

Now back to the reason we were here.

The cook leaned forward and said,

"I know one person who would be interested in working as a full-time helper for your in-laws."

Ajay asked, **"Is he trustworthy?"**

The cook nodded, **"Absolutely. He's from a good family. But his charges are slightly higher than usual."**

I wasn't surprised. Finding a reliable, known person these days is like finding gold. Most villagers migrate to cities for better opportunities.

I said, **"That's fine. If he's dependable, we're okay with the amount."**

Ajay added, **"He can stay in the extra room at my in-laws' house. It has a separate entry, so he'll have his own space."**

We discussed the role—cooking, household chores, and fetching groceries and vegetables from the nearby market. Simple, but essential.

The deal was locked. Both sides were satisfied.

My whole idea was simple: let my in-laws sit back on the couch and enjoy their days without worrying about daily chores.

Soon, we were served tea and homemade **coconut ladoos with jaggery**. The tea was strong and sweet—too sweet for me. I managed two sips before the sugar started sticking to my tongue.

But the ladoos? Irresistible. I took one, then split it in half and passed it to Ajay.

"Here, you take the other half."

He grinned, **"Gladly!"**

The taste was pure nostalgia—soft coconut, earthy jaggery, and the warmth of a home that still believes in hospitality.

As we sat there, sipping tea and sharing ladoos, I looked around at the simple house, the cattle in the courtyard, and the two daughters studying hard for a better future.

This is India—where simplicity and ambition coexist.

For a moment, I thought about my life in the U.S.—structured, fast-paced, and full of conveniences. And here I was, in a remote Jharkhand village, negotiating for a helper so my in-laws could live comfortably.

Two worlds. Both mine and I am loving it.

CHAPTER 38

GROCERIES FOR BABA, BLESSINGS FOR ME

That task taken care of, we started for Chas.

Chas—the place where my in-laws live.

I was getting constant calls from Mami, who happens to be Rupa's sister too, checking when Ajay and I would reach. It was already past 2 PM, so lunch time had slipped by. I told her it would take almost an hour. My Mamajee was also there, waiting for us.

Returning was faster this time. The area wasn't unknown anymore. We were back on the highway, and suddenly a memory flashed. The last time I visited Ajay's dairy, he had stopped his bike at a small shop, bought some groceries, and then, a few miles ahead, handed them to an old baba living alone in a temporary shed. No one to take care of him.

I was super impressed that day. I'm a similar person—I love helping people within my capacity. So this time, traveling on the same highway, I told Ajay, "Let's meet the baba."

We asked the driver to stop near a grocery store. I bought rice, daal, potatoes, and oil. Then we drove to baba's shed. He wasn't there—maybe gone somewhere. So we kept the grocery inside his shed and left quietly.

Next stop: the ancestral Kallibaari of Ajay's family. We left the highway and took a concrete road to reach the temple. No one was there at that hour. It was quiet and surreal, adding to the temple's aura.

I did the darshan with folded hands while Ajay narrated its history. Since we were getting late and my in-laws were waiting, we didn't linger. Back to the concrete road, which led us straight to their place.

Knocked on the iron door. It opened, and there stood my Mamajee. I bent down, touched his feet, and took his blessings.

Now came the time to bell the cat—my mother-in-law.

She is a very simple woman. Both my in-laws are still stuck in the 80s. Her philosophy? Nature is sacred. No trees should be chopped for highways or buildings. Land should only be used for agriculture. Not her fault—she spent most of her childhood in a village and the rest of her life in semi-urban Chas. Yes, she stayed in Bokaro Steel City for a while, but urbanization never really rubbed off on her.

We all knew she wouldn't agree to a 24×7 helper. We've tried before. Everyone failed. But this time, I was in India, and during my Rakhi trip, I realized—it's too late to ignore this. They need someone at home. Rodents were troubling them, and it was becoming a nuisance.

And these rodents? Oh, they're not ordinary. They're graduates from IIT-Rodent. My mother-in-law told me they sneak into the kitchen when no one's around, turn the lids off, and empty the food she cooks. Later, you'll find that food inside some almirah or cabinet. Once, I found aaloo bhujiya hidden inside the inverter case! The cover fell off when the maid was sweeping.They also started hiding the 'belna' – the chapati dough roller.

Now, you'll say—"Come on, controlling rodents in India is easy. Get a mousetrap, put some bait, and done." But no, these rodents have evolved. Their sixth sense screams *danger* when they see a trap. Smart, right?

I asked her, "Why don't you poison them?"

She said, "Yes, that's an option. But when they die, they prefer to die alone in some corner. If you can't find them, the whole house smells like rotten eggs."

Fair point. I had no alternative solution. And I was leaving for Ranchi the next day.

So, the only permanent fix? A full-time helper. But convincing her? Almost impossible. Everyone had given up.

Lunch was served. Ajay, Mamajee, and I sat together. Ajay had already paid the driver and sent him to a hotel for lunch. My mother-in-law sat on a chair behind me.

While eating, I turned to her and said, "Maa, we've found a full-time helper for you both. He'll stay in this room"—I pointed to the one next to the master bedroom—"and take care of everything. Grocery shopping, rodents who roam fearlessly, your plants, opening and closing the iron gate, cooking food, replacing water cans…"

I was pitching like a seasoned salesman. She listened patiently, waiting for me to finish. Then she said, "Kutu Babu"—that's what she calls me—"as long as I can walk and do my own work, we don't need help. If we stop doing anything and just sit on the couch, watch TV, and call this boy for everything, the body will start rotting."

She wasn't done. "I have to see Anshuman's wedding and Atharva's Yagopavitra Sanskar (Janeu). Maybe after five years, I'll need help."

I looked around for backup—Ajay, Mami, Mamajee. Silence. They know her better. Ajay tried, though: "Maa, we spent half a day finding this helper. Bhaiya came to Chas a second time just for this."

But she didn't budge. She's the boss in these matters. My father-in-law? He kills the topic before you finish the first sentence.

I realized there was no point dragging it. "Okay," I said. "Let's leave it this time. But promise me you'll let the current maid cook for you guys."

Even that had a logistics challenge—olden values and beliefs, well, stuck in the 80s. So, the only commitment I got was: the maid stays. At least some help.

We focused on lunch. She had made six or seven items (I suspect the paneer came from Mohan Dhaba) with rice and daal. We finished, and the driver returned with the car.

On the highway earlier, leaving groceries for a lonely baba felt sacred in its own way. Maybe life isn't about choosing between old customs and modern practicality. It's about carrying both in your heart—because blessings can come from folded hands or from a quiet act of kindness on an empty road.

CHAPTER 39

CRICKET, COMPLIMENTS, AND CONVERSATIONS

The next plan was to visit my younger sister and her in-laws, about 10 kilometers away in Chira Chas. I had been there on Rakhi day, but that visit felt incomplete—I couldn't showcase my leg-spin bowling to my nephews, Arnav and Ishu. Both play good cricket, and once, jokingly, I told Ishu, "I'll beat you with spin." That friendly rivalry was waiting to be settled.

We started for the place—Ajay and I, with the driver. Once we hit the main road, we realized the traffic wasn't moving. Not sure if there was a procession or something else. Thankfully, we found a detour through a neighbourhood and joined a parallel road. By the time we reached my sister's place, it was almost 4 PM.

I rang the bell, and my brother-in-law opened the door. It was Sunday, so he was calm and probably taking a little nap—I had disturbed that peace. The very first thing my sister said was, "Good, Bhaiya! Today you're looking young and properly dressed."

Yes, I had gotten a haircut, colored my hair, and was wearing full pants with a nice T-shirt. She was definitely pulling my leg because last time, on Rakhi, I had shown up in shorts with a grown beard. I took the compliment anyway.

Soon, her in-laws came in. I caught up with Samdhi Baba (her father-in-law). He loves talking to me—and the feeling is mutual. A retired SAIL employee, he still keeps himself busy with social work for our Sathgharia Maithil Samaj. We are Bengali-speaking Jhas with roots in Darbhanga. He confirmed my contact details since he was working on a database of like-minded people from our community.

We spent some time together, clicked a selfie, and then I noticed Ishu and Arnav were eager to go downstairs to play cricket. I said, "Let's go," and bid goodbye to Samdhi Baba.

We came downstairs, and soon a few kids from neighboring towers and flats joined us. The small ground suddenly felt alive with chatter and excitement. I marked my run-up—short, because I was planning to bowl leg-spin.

Arnav was batting first. I beat him on flight a few times, and later he adjusted—staying back, waiting for the spin to die, and then smacking me. The contest was 50:50. I got smacked, but I also beat him twice and almost had him stumped after a beautiful flighted delivery.

Ishu joined in, bowling a few balls to Arnav. His deliveries were swinging in, and because Ishu is only eight, his height made the ball skid low, adding to Arnav's challenge. It was fun watching the brothers compete.

Then came the final challenge: Ishu vs. Me. I was bowling now, and Ishu was ready. He hit a couple of good shots, no doubt, but on the fourth or fifth delivery, I bowled him. The ball pitched outside leg stump, turned sharply, and clipped the middle stump after beating him. I had slowed the pace, and Ishu played his shot early.

I was ecstatic! Ishu, of course, complained—he wanted to play more. But time wasn't on our side. Ajay and I had to leave for Ranchi, and it was already close to 6 PM.

We went back upstairs, had a quick cup of tea, and said our goodbyes. The next meeting? Probably when I visit India again—maybe next year.

From there, we headed to Sector 4 market. One of my Mamajees lives there, and I hadn't met him in years. The last time I visited his house, either they weren't home or I was knocking on the wrong door. Ajay was with me that time too.

This time, we were in front of the right door. My Mami opened it. I hadn't given any heads-up—I wanted to surprise them. I bent down and touched her feet. She was overjoyed to see me.

I asked where Mamajee was. He was in the master bedroom, recovering from fatigue caused by a heavy workout in the park yesterday. He had overdone it and even visited a doctor, but thankfully, it was just normal muscle aches. He was feeling better now.

Let me tell you more about him. His name is **Bijay Shekhar Jha**, the second oldest among my five Mamajees—the "Paanch Pandavas." Growing up, he was strict with kids (especially me) and had an intimidating personality. I vividly remember him playing the role of *Mahishasur* in one of the plays staged at my Mamaghar during Kali Puja. It was a tradition—the play would pause at midnight for the Puja and Bali.

Even now, I'm not as comfortable and friendly with him as I am with my other Mamajees. He was always brimming with energy, commanding people around. Seeing him post-retirement, slowed down by age, was hard to accept.

We caught up. He told me about their daughters ,my cousin sisters —they're in Delhi. Mami suggested that if I had time, I should meet them. I said, "Yes, Mami. When I go back to Delhi to fly to the U.S., I'll try to stop by—the elder cousin lives close to Indira Gandhi Airport."

After some snacks and coffee (though Mami insisted on dinner), we left. The plan was to visit another cousin on the way back to Ranchi, but we dropped that idea. We stopped near Naya More to buy a cold drink, Rajnigandha and two bottles of water. It was almost 7 PM when we started again.

From there, there was only one way—and that was Ranchi. Life changes quietly. The people who once seemed larger than life now speak softly, move slowly, and share stories instead of commands. It reminded me that time humbles everyone—and maybe that's its greatest lesson.

CHAPTER 40

KHALSA DHABA AND THE DAAL TADKA

The drive back was anything but dull. Ajay and I touched on everything—from his plans to stay in Ranchi or move back to Chas, to juggling his coaching job as a commerce specialist with his side hustles.

He already owns a dairy farm, which, as he put it, is running at "zero profit, zero loss."

"It just needs more commitment from all partners," he said, shaking his head.

I remembered visiting his dairy once—I was impressed by the assets, the packaging, and the expansion plans. It had promise. Consumers today crave organic milk and are willing to pay for it. All you need is quality and consistency.

Before leaving Naya More, Ajay grinned and said,

"Bhaiya, there's a dhaba in Sikidiri Ghati you must try. Their Daal Tadka and Tandoori Roti are legendary."

It was Krishna Janmashtami, so we were strictly vegetarian that day. I called Mom,

"Don't count us for dinner. We'll eat on the way. Planning to have Daal Tadka and Roti."

Honestly, I couldn't remember the last time I had that combo at a roadside dhaba.

The dhaba's name? **Khalsa Dhaba**—an icon on the old Ranchi-Ramgarh route. When the main highway was closed for construction, the Sikidiri route became the go-to. People love it for its scenic beauty and better roads.

We reached around 9:30 p.m. The drizzle made the air cool and pleasant. Khalsa Dhaba stood proudly on one side of the road, with ample parking between the highway and its steel-sheet structure.

No doors—the entire front was open to the road. Inside, it was rustic: wooden beams, high ceilings, big fans whirring lazily. No fancy décor, no frills—just rows of sturdy tables and chairs.

Ajay and I headed straight to the washroom, came back, and grabbed a table near the counter. The driver didn't join us. He was getting constant calls, and later confessed,

"Sir, my friends are waiting at the Ranchi airport parking. That's our adda after work."

I laughed, **"Good boy! But you never asked us to hurry."**

He smiled, **"I'll eat with them later. You take your time."** Professional to the core.

We ordered **Daal Tadka**—the original version, meaning no alterations, just the classic style seasoned with tempering (*tadka*), where spices sizzle in hot ghee before being poured over the lentils. Along with it came **Tandoori Roti**, a fresh **salad**, and yes, I sneaked in a two-egg omelette for myself. To top it all off, we added a refreshing **masala soda** to the order. I wished they served beer—but no alcohol here. Good for my health, I guess.

The aroma of the daal was irresistible—earthy lentils mingled with the smoky fragrance of cumin and garlic from the tempering. The ghee gave it a rich, nutty finish that made my taste buds dance even before the first bite. The rotis were warm and slightly charred at the edges, perfect for scooping up the silky daal. The salad added a crisp freshness, and the omelette, golden and fluffy, was my guilty pleasure. When the masala soda arrived, its tangy fizz was the perfect curtain call to this rustic symphony of flavors.

We polished off everything and ended with masala soda.

While leaving, I noticed the chef relaxing near the entrance, wiping his hands on a towel. Curiosity got the better of me, so I asked,

"How long have you been cooking this Daal Tadka?"

He smiled, a quiet pride in his eyes,

"Twenty years."

Twenty years of perfecting one dish. That's not just cooking—that's craftsmanship.

And here's the kicker: the man was Bengali, yet he had mastered a Punjabi classic. That, to me, is the true essence of India—diversity blending seamlessly on a plate.

Walking back to the car, we carried the traditional **saunf** in our hands. My home was still 90 minutes away—45 minutes to the Ring Road, then another 30–45 depending on which flyover was under construction.

Ranchi has grown. Every visit feels like a new city—ring roads, malls, hospitals, herbal tea points, and restaurants popping up everywhere.

By the time we reached Namkum, it was close to midnight. We had an alternate plan to stop at Harmu and pick up **Anarsa**—a sweet made of rice flour and jaggery, one of Rupa's and my favorites. Ajay had even called the guy to keep it ready.

But it was late, so I said,

"Leave it for now. I'll come to your place before leaving for the U.S. anyway."

Nishu was also sending gifts for Aarna and Anusha, so another visit was guaranteed.

At home, nothing much happened. I had a cup of tea and called it a day.

As I lay in bed that night, the hum of Ranchi's quiet streets outside, I thought about the past few days—the registry office chaos, the laughter on Arvind's balcony, the drizzle-soaked drive through Sikidiri Ghati, and that unforgettable Daal Tadka at Khalsa Dhaba.

Life in the U.S. is polished—structured, efficient, and predictable. But here? Here, it's raw, imperfect, and beautifully human. Plans change, roads twist, and conversations meander like rivers. Yet, in this unpredictability lies a warmth that no GPS or calendar invite can replicate.

Family makes you pause. Nostalgia makes you smile. And simplicity—like a tin-roof dhaba serving food cooked with love—reminds you that happiness doesn't need Michelin stars. It just needs a plate of Daal Tadka, a drizzle outside, and someone to share it with.

Two worlds. Both mine. And every time I cross oceans, I realize—I don't belong to one or the other. I belong to the bridge between them.

CHAPTER 41

ERRANDS AND LITTLE WINS

The next day was reserved for tasks that had been sitting at the bottom of my priority list for ages. Finally, I had the time.

First stop: **ICICI Bank**. I needed to update my address and mobile number and convert my account to an NRE account. Luckily, there's an ICICI branch in Namkum, barely two kilometers from home.

I drive a bike in India, but honestly, I've lost the confidence to drive a car here. The traffic feels like a video game on steroids—except there's no restart button. So, bike it was.

I reached the bank around 10 a.m. It was a brand-new branch, gleaming floors, and barely any customers—maybe because it was still early. I asked the security guard where the manager's chamber was. He politely asked me to wait, then went inside to inform her.

The manager was a lady. She welcomed me with a smile and said,

"Sir, just give me your address and phone number. I'll send my staff to your home to complete the paperwork."

Perfect. I took her card, thanked her, and walked out feeling like I'd ticked off a big item with minimal effort.

Next on the list: **exchange the dress I'd bought for Avyaa (Arvind's daughter)**. So, I hopped back on the bike and headed to Namkum market. The shop was at the main junction. I parked, climbed the stairs, and found the salesgirl.

"I need to exchange this," I explained. She smiled,

"Sure, sir. Please come to the next counter. We'll show you the options."

I wanted something party-style with pink in it. No luck—nothing with pink as the main color. But then I spotted one with yellow and pink, complete with a matching purse and a cute coat that could pair with jeans or any other dress. Perfect.

Mission accomplished. I paid the difference, packed the dress and rode back home, feeling oddly satisfied.

I was having lunch when my brother walked in from work. Now, here's the backstory: Mom had been reminding him for days that she wanted to buy a sari for Rupa and dresses for her granddaughters. The plan was that he would take her shopping.

But my brother is a busy man—and why not? He juggles **two side hustles and one primary job**, giving full commitment to all three. I've seen him working late nights, laptop open, reconciling numbers like a Wall Street analyst.

Of course, I know his secret weapon—**Ruma**, his wife. She's the backbone of the household, managing the academic side of the kids: monitoring school progress, checking journals, interacting with tuition teachers, helping with homework, and handling household chores. Honestly, salute to her.

Coming back to the story—Mom was furious. The shopping plan had been pushed so many times, and now she had switched to her "storm mode." I know that avatar well—it can get nasty for a few hours before calm returns.

So, I jumped in like a UN peacekeeper and said,

"Mom, yes, he should be sorry. This task is important too. Don't worry—I'll take you shopping. In fact, we both will."

The storm was quelled before it could turn into a full-blown cyclone.

We started from home around 3 p.m.—me, Mom, and my brother. The plan was to head to **Pantaloons in Hinoo**, a store we've always had good experiences with. I'd even been there once with Rupa, and she liked it. We had picked a dress for Aarna back then—she might still remember.

By 3:30 p.m., we were there. My brother did the classic **Indian roadside parking maneuver**. Here's the trick: if you wait for the traffic behind you to slow down, you'll never park. You just have to go for it—they'll either slow down or squeeze past you. It's a game of confidence, not courtesy.

We walked a bit and climbed the stairs to enter the store. They had escalators, but Mom wasn't comfortable with those, so we took the stairs. Soon, a salesman greeted us with a smile.

After a few minutes of browsing, we settled on the dresses we wanted. Mom insisted I buy something for myself, but I refused. The challenge? Sizes. Only XL and above. And honestly, nothing kills your mood faster than trying on a shirt in the trial room and realizing it's tight around the stomach. Hopeless feeling. So, I avoided that trap.

Mom kept insisting, but I stood firm.

"No, Mom. Let's focus on your picks."

Payment time. My brother took charge and tried applying a coupon code—but it had expired. The guy at the counter even called customer care for a one-time exception, but they refused. Finally, my brother paid the full amount, and we left.

Still, Mom had one more mission: a sari for Rupa. And I had mine—**pick up some bhunja** (roasted snacks) to carry back to the U.S. So, we headed to **Doranda Bazaar**.

First stop: **Pramila Textile**, Mom's favorite garment shop. It was the classic setup—customers seated on one side of the counter, and on the other, the salesman pulling saris from racks and spreading them out on a raised platform. Mom had already reserved one earlier, and sure enough, the third sari he showed was the one she had her eye on.

I liked it too—dark color, just Rupa's style.

"Yes, Mom. She doesn't have a sari in this shade. She'll love it."

The owner gave us special attention—he knew this sari was going abroad. Mom has been buying from this shop since the '90s, back when most purchases were on **udhaari** (credit), and payments were settled once a month. Times have changed, but loyalty hasn't.

My mom asked the shopkeeper to pack the saari and we left the shop after making the payment.Another task done.Mom is back to normal.

As we walked out of Pramila Textile with the sari neatly packed, I couldn't help but smile. These small errands—buying dresses, picking bhunja, hunting for the perfect sari—aren't just tasks. They're bonding rituals. Moments where conversations flow, laughter sneaks in, and family feels like family again.

Doranda Bazaar hasn't changed much over the years. The same narrow lanes, the same paan shop at the corner, the same chaos that somehow feels organized. Sure, there are new signboards and a few fancy LED lights, but the soul remains the same. It's comforting—like an old friend who still remembers your favorite snack.

And honestly, nothing beats the drama of shopping with Mom. From sari debates to size struggles, it's a full-fledged family episode. Amazon can deliver in one click, but it can't give you the joy of sitting on a wooden bench while someone flips saris like playing cards. That's India—and that's home.

Before heading home, we stopped at a small shop in Doranda to pick up **bhunja**—my favorite roasted snack and a must-pack item for the U.S. trip. The shop was tiny, stacked with jars of murmura, chana, peanuts, and namkeen.

I asked the shopkeeper, **"Bhaiya, give me a kilo of bhunja."**

He looked at me and said, **"Sir, one kilo won't survive Ranchi traffic, forget America."**

I laughed, **"Okay, make it three kilos then. And pack it like it's going to space."**

He grinned, pulled out a plastic bag, and started stuffing it like he was packing gold.

Watching him, I thought—this is the beauty of India. You can walk into a shop, ask for something as simple as roasted grains, and end up having a full-blown conversation about its travel plans. Try explaining that to a cashier at Walmart!

CHAPTER 42

GAMING, CRICKET SHOTS AND DINNER PLANS

By evening, I had a plan to make the kids happy—**a trip to the gaming complex**. I'd already told Nishu that if Atharva finished his homework, he could join us. Kids love gaming zones—it's their Disneyland.

Akshu and Gungun came back from school, had a late lunch, finished their homework, and were ready to roll. My brother was home too, so around 6 p.m., we started for Harmu, picked up Atharva, and headed straight to the gaming zone.

The place was inside a pretty decent mall. After parking, we went straight to the second floor where the neon lights and arcade sounds welcomed us. The kids' eyes lit up like Diwali lamps.

First stop: **VR games**—headsets on, reality off. Then came the sports bike rides, where Akshu and Atharva looked like mini MotoGP racers. But the main attraction? **The cricket zone.**

A bowling machine, adjustable speed, and a netted pitch—it was heaven for these kids. Both Akshu and Atharva tried their best to impress. Atharva even attempted a dramatic bend and slog shot, channeling his inner Ben Stokes. I laughed and said,

"Play straight, boys!"

But thanks to the evolution of T20 cricket, nobody cares about basics anymore. Every ball is a six-ball. Fundamentals? Forgotten. Entertainment? Maxed out.

While the kids were busy smashing balls, Gungun decided to try the VR roller coaster ride. She put on the headset, sat in the moving chair, and the simulation began. Within seconds, she screamed,

"Bade papa! Stop this train! I want to get down!"

The attendant and I burst out laughing. I said,

"Beta, it's not a train—it's virtual reality. You're not going anywhere!"

She kept clutching the chair like her life depended on it. When the ride ended, she pulled off the headset and declared,

"Never again! I'll stick to simple rides."

Classic moment. Worth every rupee.

After an hour of gaming, we left with happy faces and tired arms. Next mission: **dinner**. It was already late, so I asked,

"What do you guys want to eat?"

Atharva jumped in,

"Mausaji, there's one restaurant I go to on my birthday. Let's go there!"

Perfect. The restaurant was near Dhoni's old house—now converted into a super-specialty sports rehabilitation center. Dhoni himself lives on the outskirts these days, farming **Kadaknath chickens and growing vegetables**. Only in India can cricket and poultry farming share the same sentence.

We reached after battling some traffic. Everyone ordered their favorites. I was planning to head home, finish some office work, and then eat. We wrapped up dinner around 9 p.m., dropped Atharva home, and I promised Nishu,

"I'll come back before leaving for the U.S."

As we drove back, I couldn't help but chuckle. Today's kids get their adrenaline rush from VR headsets and bowling machines. Back in our day, our "gaming zone" was a dusty street, two bricks for wickets, and a tennis ball that had seen better days. No neon lights, no joystick—just pure chaos and creativity. And guess what? We still thought we were playing for India.

CHAPTER 43

THE LAST-MINUTE MARATHON

It was **19th August**, and my flight to Delhi was booked for tomorrow afternoon. I had exactly **one day** to finish everything—shopping, packing, and solving the puzzle of airline baggage limits.

Rupa had asked Mom to buy some essentials—**utensils, sattu, and the famous 'jhaal' mixture** (Anusha's favorite). On top of that, I had to pack all the gifts from aunts, uncles, and cousins for Aarna and Anusha.

And then came the big problem: **baggage allowance**. Ranchi to Delhi is a domestic flight, so only **one bag allowed**, with a weight limit of **15 kg**. The suitcase itself weighs 3–4 kg! There was no way everything would fit.

That's when Subrata came to the rescue with a brilliant idea:

"Bhaiya, since your final destination is international and within 48 hours, you can buy the international baggage option."

For ₹3,000, I could get an extra 20 kg and carry a second bag. Perfect! If I had paid per kg for being overweight, the airline would have charged ₹500–600 per kg—not worth it for the stuff I was carrying. So, while booking the Ranchi–Delhi flight, I added the extra allowance. Crisis averted.

Next, I had to ensure all **immigration paperwork, passports (old and new)**, and the **medicines Sandy and Brajesh (my buddies in US)**

had asked for were ready. My mind was juggling tasks like a circus performer.

Just then, I got a call from ICICI Bank—the staff was on her way to complete the paperwork for converting my account to NRE, updating my address, and phone number. After some guidance from my brother, she arrived—a young, confident girl. Honestly, it was refreshing to see women taking on roles traditionally dominated by men. She took my signatures, explained the process, and left. Another box ticked.

Back to packing. Somehow, I managed to squeeze everything within the limit—but the bags were still slightly overweight. I told Mom,

"I'll take a chance."

In the evening, I headed to Nishu's house to collect more gifts for the kids in the U.S. Could I say no? Of course not. Ajay was back from coaching and had already arranged **Anarsa** from the famous shop. More luggage. More stress.

With all this extra baggage, I booked an Ola and returned home. Finally, I sat with family, watched a few episodes of *Taarak Mehta Ka Ooltah Chashmah* on YouTube, had dinner, and called it a day.

CHAPTER 44

THE WEIGHT OF GOODBYES

The morning was a blur of last-minute packing and weighing bags like a nervous contestant on a reality show. I still had **2–3 extra kilos** spread across the two suitcases. Then there was my laptop bag—stuffed beyond recognition with documents and a few books I'd bought at Delhi Airport earlier. The poor laptop was buried under layers of paper and hardcovers. No more room for anything else.

I did a final check, took a quick bath, and got ready. My flight was at **3:15 p.m.**, so I had to be at the airport by **2:00 p.m.** and leave home no later than **1:30 p.m.** Thankfully, Ranchi airport is close to home.

Before leaving, I sat down for **one last lunch at home** this trip. Mom and Ruma had made my favorites—**rice, daal, begun bhaja, and postu**. I savored every bite, knowing it would be months before I tasted this again. Across the table, Mom wore that familiar sad expression—the one that says more than words ever could. In a few minutes, I'd be leaving.

The kids were at school and hadn't returned yet. They'd left before I woke up, so no goodbyes today. That stung a little.

With a heavy heart, I hugged Mom and Dad , said my goodbyes, and stepped into the car. My brother started the engine. I looked out the window, trying to capture everything—the drizzle, the green patches, the familiar chaos of Ranchi roads—into memory.

We reached the airport on time. As expected, the baggage drama wasn't over. I told my brother to wait near the departure gate—Ranchi airport is small, so that's allowed. Big airports would have shooed him away in two minutes flat.

I showed my ID and entered. My flight was with **IndiGo**, so I headed straight to the check-in counter and asked for a window seat. The agent smiled and obliged.

Then came the moment of truth—the weighing machine. One bag was within the limit. The other? **Overweight by 6 kilos**. That meant shelling out ₹3,000–₹4,000 extra. The irony? The stuff wasn't worth that much in money—but in emotion, it was priceless. **Sattu and jhaal mixture**—local treasures you can't find in Delhi, let alone the U.S.

I explained this to the check-in guy. He nodded sympathetically and said,

"Sir, I can't check in overweight baggage without fees. But here's a tip—transfer 6 kilos into a separate bag and carry it as cabin baggage."

Brilliant. I wasn't carrying a cabin bag, so I improvised. Pulled out a spare bag, stuffed it with the extra weight, and made it my carry-on. Not elegant—the bag was flimsy, and one handle broke—but better than paying a fortune.

With that sorted, I headed to security and then the departure gate, clutching my overstuffed "carry-on" like a lifeline.

CHAPTER 45

₹450 TEA AND THE NEW INDIA

The waiting area was packed. Every seat taken, people buzzing around with luggage and smartphones. I thought of getting a cup of tea to kill time. Walked to the counter, looked at the menu, and came back empty-handed. Two reasons:

First, it wasn't sugar-free.

Second, it was ₹450 for a machine-made cup of tea.

₹450 for tea? My middle-class brain screamed, *"No way!"*

But later, I changed my mind. Bought that overpriced tea. Took two sips—too sweet for my taste—and left the rest.

Now you'll ask, *"Why did you change your mind?"*

Peer pressure. That's why. Everyone around me was happily sipping tea, coffee, slurping noodles, munching samosas. Nobody seemed to care about the price. I was thinking, *"What a waste of money!"* But clearly, I was in the minority.

This is the new India. Not the India I left 13 years ago.

One big difference I notice—people's spending power has skyrocketed. Standards of living have upgraded. For me, flying out of Ranchi Airport feels like an achievement. For others, it's just another Friday evening.

When I was studying in Trichy, Tamil Nadu, we came home twice a year. Sleeper class. Second AC was a luxury, only if the company paid. My first flight ticket? Also company-sponsored.

But now? Times have changed. Many travelers are students or young professionals. They fly home on Friday evening and return to Delhi or Bangalore by Sunday night. For them, time matters more than money.

Why this change? Are people earning more? Or just spending more? One thing is clear—the old 'saving' mentality is gone. Money is flowing. And that's good for the economy.

I bought some handicrafts from the terminal and headed to board. Another observation—boarding culture.

As soon as the crew announces, *"Aircraft is ready to board,"* people jump up and queue. Doesn't matter if their group hasn't been called yet. They just want to get in early. Why? No clue. The flight won't leave without them.

I used to enjoy watching this scene. And it's not just Ranchi. Same story in Chennai, Bangalore, Delhi—everywhere.

Finally, the plane took off.

I was in the window seat, and I kept looking outside for a long, long time. The city lights faded, the green fields turned into patches, and then clouds swallowed everything.

It will be months—maybe a year—before I come back to Ranchi. So I wanted to capture as much as I could and preserve it in memory.

There was a strange mix of emotions—gratitude, nostalgia, and a quiet realization that life keeps moving. Ranchi will wait. But will I remain the same when I return?

CHAPTER 46

TRAFFIC TALES AND A JHARKHAND CONNECTION

The plane landed around 5 PM. By the time I collected my luggage, stepped out, and booked a taxi, it was already 6 PM.

Not a good day for traffic. The roads were jam-packed—cars, buses, bikes—barely moving. At one point, we were almost at a standstill near the Prime Minister's residence.

I got a close look at the complex. Huge. Multiple entry gates. Layers of security. Armed personnel everywhere.

To kill time, I started chatting with the cab driver. He was a veteran in Delhi—20 years in this job. Originally from Godda, Jharkhand.

"Any plans to go back?" I asked.

He smiled. "Not now, sir. As long as I'm earning."

But during the COVID-19 lockdown, he had returned to Jharkhand. Spent a few years there. Worked at a thermal power plant when Adani Group was setting it up.

He wasn't just a driver then—he was a labor supervisor. Even tried his hands on construction tools like mixers.

Then came the interesting part—his stories about Chinese engineers hired for the project. Their work culture, their food habits. "They work hard," he said, "but eat things we don't even think of eating in India."

He knew all the details because everything going in or out of the Chinese camp was logged in a register. "I knew who and what was coming inside, and who and what was going outside," he said with a grin.

After hitting NH-24, I asked him to stop for tea. By now, I had developed a habit of chewing Rajnigandha, so that was another reason for the break.

This trip had its own quirks. I only had my U.S. phone with me. No Ruma's phone. So, I couldn't call Arvind to say I was running late.

To make matters worse, when I messaged Arvind and Tapan Bhaiya about my return, I wrote, "Flight at 3 o'clock." But didn't clarify whether that was departure or arrival.

It was departure. The flight landed in Delhi at 5 PM. My bad.

They were worried, calling each other for updates. Meanwhile, I was unreachable because my phone was practically useless here.

Realizing this, I asked the cab driver if I could use his phone. "No problem, sir," he said.

I called Arvind first, then Tapan Bhaiya. Told them I'd reach around 8 PM.

Got a good dose from both. I deserved it.

That ride was more than just a commute. It was a reminder of how life connects in unexpected ways—a Jharkhand cabbie in Delhi, stories of Chinese engineers, and me stuck in traffic chewing Rajnigandha.

And yes, communication matters. Next time, I'll clarify departure vs. arrival. Lesson learned.

CHAPTER 47

INDIRAPURAM NIGHTS: KEBABS, BEER AND CONVERSATIONS

It was around 9 PM when I finally stood in front of **Tower 10**. Yes, Tower 10. I went straight through Gate 3—or maybe Gate 5—the one for visitor cars, and headed to Arvind's flat.

My luggage was manageable, but those extra 6–7 kilos and a box of Haldiram sweets made it tricky. One handle had already broken at Ranchi Airport, so dragging the bags was a mini workout.

Just as I reached the lift, I saw Arvind coming from the basement. He had parked his car after dropping Aavya at her *nani's(Grandmother)* place.

"Oh no," I said. "I'll miss her!"

Later, I did a video call with her. She spoke to me for a bit but was too engrossed in the lively atmosphere there. I told her, "I've got your new dress, so try it when you're back."

Seema was still on her way from the office. Shalini was home and made tea for us. I teased her, "So, how is Aavya treating you?" (Just pulling her leg.)

Arvind asked, "So, what's the plan?"

I said, "I'm eating non-veg today. My plan was to sit in a bar, have a couple of beers with chicken snacks."

Then I added, "Let's call Tapan Bhaiya too."

I called him—needed to inform him I'd reached safely and was staying at Arvind's tonight. But I promised Himanshi Bhabhi that I'd have lunch at their place tomorrow. She even agreed to make *kadi* for me.

Tapan Bhaiya said he was done with dinner. "No worries, Bhaiya," I said. "I'll come in the morning before you leave for office. We'll have breakfast together if possible."

Back to Arvind and me—we decided to pick up some starters since we had leftover Bira beers from our last balcony party.

We strolled down and crossed over to Windsor Market—the most famous food hub in Indirapuram, and equally notorious for its liquor shop (*Theka*). It's the kind of place where "Car-O-Bar" is a weekend ritual—people sipping drinks in parked cars, turning the road into a mini party zone and, of course, a traffic nightmare.

Arvind laughed and told me how one day the chaos was so bad he had to park on this side of the road and walk all the way across to his society gate like a stranded traveler.

Today, traffic was normal. We hopped across the road like bunnies.

On the other side of the road, it was a completely different world—the world of food.

Everywhere you looked, there was something tempting: **Lucknawi kebabs**, **Karim's mutton rogan josh**, creamy chicken, galawati kebabs, Tunday Kababi, Chinese stir-fries, momos, ice creams—you name it, they had it.

When choices are endless, confusion is guaranteed. Or worse—**FOMO**.

We stood there for a good ten minutes, debating like two judges on a food reality show. Finally, after a lot of "Should we? Shouldn't we?" I settled for a takeaway of **chilli chicken** and **galawati kebabs**.

Beer? No need. We had Bira waiting at home from the last balcony party.

So, we crossed the road again and walked back into Arvind's society—ATS. The central park looked serene under the night sky, with big trees and open spaces. A few kids were still playing, their laughter echoing in the cool air.

By the time we reached his flat, Seema was home but still glued to an office call.

Between bites and sips, we drifted into our usual "big ideas" zone—like turning the balcony into a private party space with one push of a button and temperature control.

Some ideas are just ideas. You forget them by morning.

We talked about everything—work, family, random memories—and finally had dinner. Called it a day.

It was a weekday, after all. I was on vacation, but Arvind and Seema had office the next morning. That night wasn't about kebabs or beer—it was about the comfort of old friendships, the kind that makes you laugh at crazy ideas and forget the world outside.

CHAPTER 48

BREAKFAST PROMISES AND KADI DREAMS

Next morning, I woke up early, got ready, and rushed downstairs—without even a sip of water. I had promised Tapan Bhaiya, *"Breakfast with you, no excuses."*

I grabbed an auto and reached his place in no time—it was hardly a few miles away. Entered through the main gate after signing the visitor register, made my way to his tower, and finally his floor.

I rang the bell. Bhaiya opened the door—almost ready for office and waiting for me.

Straight to the breakfast table. Himanshi Bhabhi had laid out a spread—poha, a chana-moong salad, and some fresh fruits. Simple, healthy, and satisfying.

Bhaiya finished quickly and was ready to leave. Before heading out, he dropped me near a shop where I planned to buy sattu to carry back to the U.S. But I was too early—the shop was closed. My watch showed 9 AM.

I checked with a nearby *paan* shop guy. He said, "Opens late." So, I postponed the plan and headed back to Arvind's place.

Yes, I had promised Himanshi Bhabhi I'd return for lunch if she made kadi-chawal. She was more than happy to say yes.

Back at Arvind's, I had no major tasks except buying sattu, sweets, and some medicines—including antibiotics.

I cross-checked my travel documents, took a bath, and got ready for my next errand—**HDFC Bank**.

My plan at the bank was simple but important: check the details of my NRE account, confirm address and phone number update and initiate the home loan discussion. I wanted to get the process rolling and reach a stage where the loan was **disbursal-ready** before heading back to the U.S.

At the bank, I met my Bihari friend and his boss. Same warm treatment as always. They introduced me to the home loan point of contact. We exchanged numbers, and he sent me a list of required documents on WhatsApp. I'd share those once back in the U.S.

I also got updates on other pending activities. Thanked them and left.

From there, I took an e-rickshaw to **Saya Gold Avenue**—Tapan Bhaiya's housing complex. By now, the security guards recognized me, so they waved me in without the usual drill.

I went straight to his tower, took the lift, and rang the bell. This time, **Tiya** opened the door—their younger daughter.

She's a lovely girl, just finished high school and ready to start college. She welcomed me warmly, and I settled on the sofa.

We chatted about her college plans. She said she was super excited. I wished her all the best.

Tiya feels like my own daughter—I've seen her take baby steps. She used to spend so much time with me and Rupa. She called me **"Tantan"**—music to my ears then, and even now.

Soon, Bhabhi came out and said, "Bhaiya, food is almost ready. Come and sit."

I obliged. Tiya was doing all the serving, helping her mom like a pro. I was super impressed.

I filled my plate and enjoyed every bite—especially the **kadi-chawal**.

To keep the conversation going, I asked, "Tiya beta, did you watch *Saiyara*?" (It was the craze among teens then.)

She said, "Yes, Uncle, but I didn't like it as much as others."

Then she narrated the whole story—the ups and downs, the twists, and the emotional climax. It was a roller coaster indeed.

We talked about other things too. I gave her some *gyaan* on coping with engineering college life.

Finally, I finished lunch, thanked both of them, and took leave. Till now the day was about promises kept, warm conversations and the simple joy of home-cooked food. Sometimes, happiness is just a plate of kadi-chawal and a chat with someone who still calls you "Tantan."

CHAPTER 49

THE COUNTDOWN BEGINS

I came back to Arvind's house. It was empty—Arvind and Seema were at work, Aavya was at her *Nani's* place, and Shalini had stepped out for groceries.

I settled on the bed for a quick power nap. Don't remember when I slipped into slumber, but when I woke up, it was almost 6 PM.

My flight was at **4:20 AM**, and I needed to be at the airport at least three hours early. So, the plan was to leave by **11:30 PM**. That gave me about five and a half hours to wrap up pending shopping and get ready.

One of my checked-in bags was almost ready—the stuff I carried from Ranchi. I had left another bag at Arvind's place before going to Ranchi, which had items from my first visit that needed to go back to the U.S.

I spread everything on the bed in the room I'd been using for the past few days. The AC in that room was funny—it had stopped showing the temperature display, so adjusting it was pure guesswork.

I called Tapan Bhaiya to check if he was back from office. He was, and said, "Come over."

So, I pulled the empty suitcase and left Arvind's home for Tapan Bhaiya's flat.

When I reached, I asked Bhabhi to make some tea because I had to step out to buy medicines—some for me and some for friends and their parents in the U.S.

But Bhaiya said, "Come on, Debashis, just sit and enjoy tea and snacks. I'll make sure the medicines are delivered here."

I said, "Great, Bhaiya! That's one big item off my list."

He asked me to WhatsApp the list and quantities. I did, and he forwarded it to a nearby medical shop and even called them to confirm urgency.

I called Arvind to tell him I was at Tapan Bhaiya's place so he could join me later. The idea was to finish the last-minute shopping with him—and use his car to carry everything.

He said he'd come soon but was stuck in Delhi's peak evening traffic.

Meanwhile, I enjoyed tea and snacks like a king.

In between, Bhaiya got a call from the medical shop—the guy said he was short on one medicine. I said, "Perfectly fine."

About an hour later, the delivery guy showed up with the medicines. By then, Arvind had also arrived and was enjoying the hospitality.

I took the medicines, paid the bill, and ticked another task off my list. Perfect.

CHAPTER 50

PACKING SURPRISES AND VIDEO CALLS

By the time I looked at the clock, it was almost **9 PM**—the countdown had officially begun.

I asked Himanshi Bhabhi, "Bhabhi, please get the stuff Rupa ordered online and shipped here."

She nodded and started bringing boxes—one by one. At least **five boxes** landed on the bed.

I opened the suitcase and waited like a customs officer inspecting goods.

Inside the boxes? **Indian ethnic dresses** for Rupa and my daughters, Aarna and Anusha. That part I could guess. But then came the surprise—**craft items**. And not just a few—almost **100 pieces**!

I stared at them, clueless. "What is all this?"

Made a video call to Rupa—it was early morning in **San Antonio, USA**. She picked up, we exchanged greetings, and then I asked, "Mom, what is this stuff and why in so much quantity?"

She laughed and explained—they were for **return gifts** at Aarna's upcoming **16th birthday**.

I had no choice but to pack them all.

Bhabhi and Tiya helped me stuff everything into the suitcase. I zipped it up, lifted it onto the weighing machine, and sighed with relief—it still had a few kilos of room.

Good. Because I still needed to buy **sattu** and **Indian sweets**.

Dragging the suitcase behind me, I bid goodbye to Tapan Bhaiya, Himanshi Bhabhi, and Tiya one more time—with the usual promise, *"Will visit again soon."*

Arvind was with me, and I told him, "Bro, we have to pick up the sattu first."

Tapan Bhaiya had already called ahead and given a heads-up to the **chakki guy** who sells fresh sattu. I remembered the shop and the brand name—**Tathastu**. The shopkeeper knew we were coming and was waiting for us before closing for the day.

This shop was close to my old flat—the one I had just sold a few days back. A little nostalgia hit me as we drove past.

We reached the shop in Arvind's car. The guy was literally switching off the lights, ready to shut down. I quickly picked up **2 kilos of sattu** and left.

Next stop—**Mithas in Niti Khand**, the sweet shop. I had bought sweets from there before, and the quality never disappoints.

I recalculated my baggage allowance like a mathematician under pressure and figured I could squeeze in **4 kilos of sweets**.

Now came the real dilemma—what to pick? It felt like standing in front of a jewelry counter, except everything was edible and dripping with ghee.

I told the shopkeeper, "Bhaiya, make two boxes with a mix—laddoos, barfi, kaju katli." Basically, the greatest hits of Indian sweets.

For the third box, I went classic—**motichoor laddoos**, because if laddoos were a Bollywood hero, motichoor would be Amitabh Bachchan.

And the fourth? **Doda barfi**—because every box needs that one underrated character actor who steals the show.

I paid the bill, feeling like I had just curated a gourmet art exhibit, and we drove back to Arvind's home.

CHAPTER 51

UBER XL AND THE MIDNIGHT ESCAPE

By the time we reached Arvind's place, it was **10 PM**. My plan was to leave by **11:30 PM**, so I'd reach the airport around midnight—giving me a solid **four hours** for check-in, security, and maybe some last-minute airport shopping (books, medicines, or whatever catches my eye).

That meant I had **one hour** to finish packing, get ready, call the cab, and leave.

I entered the room and saw the stuff I had left out earlier. Honestly, I had been discounting this luggage while calculating how many kilos of sweets I could buy. This **last-minute miscalculation** hit me like a plot twist in a thriller.

So, I opened both bags and started rearranging things like a contestant in a reality show where the prize is "No Excess Baggage Fee."

I pulled some snacks from the big suitcase and shoved them into the cabin bag. Most of the time, airline staff don't weigh cabin bags—so I was taking that chance. I knew mine was overweight by **4–5 kilos**, but hey, optimism is free.

Even after all this juggling, my checked-in bags were still a few kilos overweight. I did my best to remove anything that wasn't a priority.

Seema joined the mission, helping me figure out what else could be shifted. I had bought some books from Delhi Airport earlier and kept them in my cabin bag. Took them out and sneaked them into my laptop bag.

Now, my laptop bag looked **pregnant**—ready to deliver twins.

Finally, I had to part ways with one bag of **bhunja**—my top priority snack. With a heavy heart, I told Seema, "You keep it."

She knew it's impossible to get this in the U.S., but she agreed. I consoled myself thinking, *At least she'll enjoy it. And honestly, finding bhunja in Delhi NCR isn't easy either.*

After this emotional farewell to bhunja, I zipped up the bags. Still overweight by a few kilos, but at this point, I left it to fate.

It was almost **11:30 PM**, so I booked an **Uber XL**—because I now had:

- **2 checked-in bags**
- **1 cabin bag**
- **1 laptop bag**

Aavya was still at her Nani's place, so saying goodbye to Arvind and Seema was easy. If Aavya had been here, it would've been tough to explain why Uncle was leaving.

Arvind and Seema came downstairs to see me off. The cab was waiting. The driver helped load the luggage.

I gave Arvind and Seema a final hug, got into the back seat, and as the cab pulled away from **Tower 10**, I saw them waving behind me. That moment—watching them wave—hit differently. Bags packed with sweets, sattu and memories. Some overweight, some priceless.

CHAPTER 52

NH-24, ABDUL AND A CUP OF CHAI

Soon, we were cruising on **NH-24**, and thankfully, traffic was moving at a normal pace. I struck up a conversation with the driver as we crossed **Khoda Colony** on our left.

Khoda Colony—one of Asia's largest labor colonies—sits on the border of Ghaziabad and Noida, adjacent to East Delhi. A densely packed urban jungle, famous for its sheer size and hustle.

I asked him, "Do you know Khoda is famous worldwide?"

He smiled, "Haan, Sir. I live here with my family—my dad and younger brother."

His name was **Abdul**. He told me his younger brother studies and also drives the cab in the morning, while Abdul mostly picks rides at night.

"Wow, that's interesting," I said.

Abdul shared more—his father came here as a laborer from a different district in UP. Over time, they bought land and built their own house.

I asked, "How many kids do you have? Do they study?"

He replied proudly, "Two kids. Both go to an English-medium school in Indirapuram."

Then he added with a grin, "My cousins have four or five kids, but I was disciplined in family planning."

I laughed and said, "Good call!" Honestly, I was impressed—his commitment to work, his focus on education, his sense of responsibility.

This was the India that touched me—people who migrate for work, build a life from scratch, and ensure their kids get a better future.

I told him, "Your story is inspiring. This should be the story of anyone who moves to a new place for work."

And then I reflected—*Who knows this better than me?* Born in Ranchi, studied in Trichy, first job in Bangalore, then Noida, then USA, back to Bangalore, and again USA. Migration is my middle name.

As we neared the airport, I asked, "Can we stop for tea?"

I wanted to savor roadside tea one last time on this trip. Abdul obliged and pulled over.

I got down, invited him to join, but he politely refused and stayed in the car. I finished my tea quickly and returned.

Within minutes, we were inside **Indira Gandhi International Airport** campus. It was buzzing with activity. Tall light towers cast a milky white glow as far as my eyes could see.

After a quick security check, we reached **Terminal A**.

I got down, pulled a luggage cart, and Abdul helped me load the bags. I paid him in cash—my only option—and thanked him sincerely.

Then, with a deep breath, I pushed my luggage toward the **International Departure Gate**. That cab ride wasn't just a commute—it was a reminder of hard work,resilience, migration, and dreams. Abdul's story mirrored mine in a way. Different paths, same spirit.

CHAPTER 53

CHECK-IN DRAMA AND SILENT PRAYERS

I showed my passport and travel ticket on my phone at the entry gate and stepped inside the terminal.

Next mission: **check-in**.

I asked an airport staff member which counter was for Indigo flights. Yes, my first leg was Indigo—Delhi to Doha. After that, Qatar Airways would take me home.

He pointed me to **Counter G**. I made my way there and joined the queue, feeling a little nervous. My bags were still overweight—especially the cabin bag. My laptop bag was stuffed and looked ready to burst like a pressure cooker.

After zig-zagging through the stanchions (those posts with retractable belts that make you feel like you're in a maze), my turn finally came.

The check-in staff turned out to be an Odiya guy—I guessed from his surname. So, I decided to break the ice:

"Are you from Odisha?"

He smiled, "Yes, Sir."

I jumped in with my classic compliment: "I have so many Odiya friends from my college days. You folks are some of the nicest people—and let's not forget, absolute champions when it comes to loving non-veg!"

He grinned, probably wondering if this was a check-in counter or a cultural appreciation seminar.

That helped. He started the process, and I asked, "Any chance of a window seat?" My plan was to lean against the window and sleep through the flight.

No luck. He offered me an aisle seat instead. "Works," I said.

Then came the moment of truth—**weighing the bags**.

First bag: **4 kg overweight**.

Second bag: just within the limit.

He looked at me, smiled, and said, "It's okay, Sir. I'll allow it without charging extra."

I thanked him silently and loudly. Looks like the ice-breaking worked.

Meanwhile, I was praying he wouldn't ask to weigh the cabin bag. That thing was a ticking time bomb—easily **4–5 kg overweight**.

Thank God, he didn't.

He handed me the boarding pass and luggage tags. I slipped them into my waist pouch along with the passport, thanked him, and walked toward **security check**, dragging my overweight cabin bag like a guilty secret.

CHAPTER 54

THE ROYAL WALK AT SECURITY CHECK

The security check area was a madhouse. Long queues snaked across the floor—peak hour for international travelers. The air buzzed with chatter, the clatter of trays, and the occasional announcement echoing through the terminal.

Families, students, and elderly folks filled the line—each with their own story. Some were off to reunite with children and grandchildren abroad, others chasing degrees in foreign lands. I stood there, wondering: *How many people take off every single day?* The sheer scale of movement felt surreal.

Two young students stood ahead of me—a boy and a girl, both clearly Gen Zs. I caught bits of their conversation and pieced together that they studied in Canada. Nothing unusual there; studying abroad is practically mainstream now. But then the boy said something that made me pause:

"I'm planning to move to Europe after my studies. You should join me if you're interested."

The confidence in his voice was striking. At his age, I was thrilled about my first solo long distance train ride from Ranchi to Bangalore.That time I was travelling to Bangalore to join my first job post Engineering. These kids? They're globe-trotting, plotting careers across continents. The world has shrunk. Accessibility has exploded. *Sky is the limit,* and they know it.

The queue crawled forward. I killed time observing people, playing silent judge of airport fashion choices. Finally, my turn came to unload belongings onto the tray—laptop, belt, wallet—the usual ritual. I joined the line for the metal detector, doing that awkward shuffle everyone does, praying any leftover coins or the locket chains doesn't trigger alarms.

That's when I saw them—a mother-daughter duo ahead of me. And oh boy, the mom looked straight out of a Bollywood period drama. Picture this: pearls, regal posture, and an aura that screamed *Rajmata has arrived!* For a second, I wondered if I'd stumbled into royalty. Maybe I was about to share an X-ray tray with someone who had a palace waiting back home.

The daughter? Equally impressive. Sweet as a box of motichoor laddoos—or maybe German chocolate, take your pick. Eternal,Elegant, confident, walking like she owned the terminal. If there were awards for "Best Airport Walk," she'd win hands down.

My turn came. Security check done. And then came one of those small, human touches that make airports less mechanical. As I stepped onto the dais for the pat-down, the officer glanced at my boarding pass, saw my name, and smiled:

"Aur Jhaji wapas ja rahe hain?"*(Heading back to Jhaji?)*

I grinned. "Yes, I work there, so I have to go."

He smiled back, handed me the pass. I thanked him, collected my cabin bag and other stuff from the X-ray tray, and walked toward the terminal gate—another tiny moment tucked into the big journey.

CHAPTER 55

LIP BALM, ANTIBIOTICS & A HERO CAMEO

I had a solid two hours before boarding began—enough time to explore the airport like a hero in an interval scene. First stop: the cosmetic shop. Mission? Buy something for my daughters. My elder one, Aarna, is so fond of cosmetics that we practically need a separate warehouse at home for her beauty arsenal.

The shop was managed by a young girl—professional, poised, and smiling like a brand ambassador in a Lakmé ad. I asked her to help me pick something for my daughters. She recommended lip balms—"easy to carry," she said, with the confidence of someone who knows her craft. I couldn't resist asking what she had studied. Her answer surprised me:

"Cosmetology. This is my full-time job."

I was impressed. Complimented her professionalism and added, "You're one sweet girl. God bless you." She smiled, and for a moment, it felt like a heartwarming scene from a slice-of-life Bollywood film—simple, genuine, and full of respect.

Next stop: the medical shop. My plan was to buy a couple of strips of antibiotics. In the U.S., you can't buy antibiotics off the shelf—they're strictly prescription-only. But in India? We're our own doctors, popping pills like extras in a Govinda comedy. Not debating whether that's good or bad—just stating the cultural contrast.

I asked the guy at the counter for two strips. While he was billing, an uncle in his 60s walked in and casually asked for a pack of condoms. My mind instantly went full Bollywood gossip mode: *Thailand trip? Goa adventure? Or just a bold hero living life king-size?* The attendant handed me my bill, and I paid in cash—again. Exit scene.

By now, my cabin baggage and laptop bag were making me feel like a porter in a vintage railway movie. I needed water. Spotted a vending machine near the gate area—hallelujah! Walked up, read the instructions, and realized the machine wanted exact change. The bottle cost ₹40. My wallet? ₹100 and ₹500 notes. I thought, *Fine, I'll buy two bottles—₹80.* But nope, the machine was stubborn. Lowest denomination I had was ₹100. Plan failed. Cue sad violin music.

I was about to give up when—like a miracle cameo—a gentleman appeared. A foreigner, Middle Eastern by the look of him. He asked if I needed help. I said, "No, I'm fine," but he saw the ₹100 note and understood the situation instantly. Without a word, he pulled out two twenty rupees notes from his wallet, bought a bottle, and handed it to me.

I was speechless. Didn't expect this from a stranger. He smiled and said:

"It's completely fine. Have a safe travel."

And just like that, he walked away—no drama, no expectation. A real-life hero moment. I stood there, holding that bottle, thinking: *Humanity is still alive. There are enough good people in this world.* Sometimes, the smallest gestures feel like the biggest scenes.

Finally, it was time to board. The announcement came like a director's cue: *"Passengers for Flight XYZ, please proceed for boarding."* I picked up my cabin bag and laptop bag—still feeling like a junior artist carrying props—and joined the line.

I stepped inside the aircraft, and the vibe changed to a cozy family drama. People settling in, struggling with overhead bins, kids running around like extras in a comedy scene. I found my seat, stuffed my bags, and sat down with a sigh .

CHAPTER 56

MY MOMENT OF REFLECTION – THE PULSE OF A NEW INDIA

As the plane started taxiing, I looked out of the window and watched the runway lights sparkle like stars, as if the stage was set for my moment of reflection.

When I look back at the India I grew up in, I remember dusty roads that told stories of neglect—potholes big enough to swallow a motorbikes, railway stations that felt like relics of another era, and airports that were more chaos than comfort. Those memories now feel like matte-finish postcards compared to the glossy present.

Multi-lane expressways slice through the countryside like silver ribbons. Airports gleam with glass and steel. Railway terminals proudly flaunt escalators, and metro trains glide silently beneath cities that once choked on traffic. This isn't just infrastructure—it's ambition cast in concrete and steel.

But the real transformation? It's in the people. Walk into any café in Bengaluru or Gurugram, and you'll see young professionals tapping away on laptops, sipping cold brews, and talking about startups, AI, studying abroad and global markets. Spending capacity has soared—not just in malls and e-commerce carts, but in dreams. Families that once saved every rupee for emergencies now plan vacations to Bali or Dubai. The middle class is no longer just surviving; it's thriving.

Digital India isn't a slogan anymore—it's a way of life. From vegetable vendors accepting UPI payments to grandmothers video-calling their grandchildren abroad, technology has seeped into every pore of society. Villages that once waited for letters now track deliveries on apps. I remember playing cricket with Arnav and Ishu, and between overs, they were talking about their YouTube channels and American football.

"Maama," Ishu said, adjusting his bat handle, "do you know how much a gaming laptop costs? I'm saving for one."

I laughed. "When I was your age, I was saving for a second-hand bicycle."

He grinned. "Times have changed, Mamajee."

Yes, they have.

And then there's the cultural shift—a quiet revolution that speaks louder than any policy. Women today aren't just participating; they're leading. They speak their minds in boardrooms, classrooms, and living rooms. I've seen it in my own family—my mother, once confined by a patriarchal society, now runs our entire household in Ranchi and negotiates terms with the confidence of a seasoned manager. And her story isn't unique—it reflects a change sweeping across countless homes in India.

It's not just the big cities anymore. People in tier-2 and tier-3 towns are jumping into the digital wave with both feet. College kids in Ranchi and Bokaro are making Instagram reels that go viral overnight. Homemakers in Bhubaneswar are running cooking channels on YouTube and earning more than they ever imagined. Even farmers are sharing videos about organic farming and finding buyers directly through social media. And then there are creators in regional languages—Bhojpuri, Marathi, Tamil—turning local culture into global conversations. Teenagers are posting tutorials on fitness, gaming, and coding, and brands are lining up to collaborate. What used to feel like a distant dream is now just a smartphone away.

CHAPTER 57

THE WORLD IS WATCHING

This transformation hasn't gone unnoticed. Global investors and Rating agencies now see India not as a risky bet but as a growth engine. Tech giants set up innovation hubs and AI datacenters here and international media often calls India the "bright spot" in the global economy. Friends from abroad tell me how their companies are looking to India for talent, not just cost savings. Even in casual conversations during my travels, I've sensed a shift—from curiosity to respect.

India's digital leap has stunned many. While some developed nations still rely on card swipes, India embraced instant mobile payments at scale. The world marvels at how a billion people adapted so quickly. And culturally, the narrative is changing too. Indian films, fashion and voices are finding global platforms. Women-led startups are making headlines and social media amplifies stories of resilience and innovation.

CHAPTER 58

THE GREAT INDIAN CIVIC SENSE – OR THE LACK OF IT

Let's be honest—Indians are champions at keeping their homes spotless. Marble floors shining, curtains matching the sofa, everything Instagram-ready. But step outside? Suddenly, the street becomes a dumping ground for garbage. It's like we believe civic sense ends at the front door.

Traffic? Oh, that's a full-blown Bollywood action scene. Honking like background music, cars zigzagging like stunt doubles, and patience? Missing in action. We talk loudly on phones in public places—because why should only the person on the other end hear our life story? Let the whole world enjoy the drama!

Queues? What queues? We treat them like optional side characters. Why wait for your turn when you can jump ahead and play the hero? And yes, we love putting our nose in other people's business—because in India, privacy is just a concept, not a practice.

Street vendors? They occupy one-third of the road. The next one-third is for parked cars. So what's left for driving? A single lane that feels like a Formula 1 track. And if there's an accident? Forget resolving it calmly. We turn the road into a live-action fight sequence, complete with shouting, gesturing, and blocking traffic for miles.

Here's my take: if we Indians get **self-disciplined and honest with ourselves**, most of these problems will solve themselves. No big policy, no magic wand—just a little patience, a little respect for rules, and a lot less drama. We should walk the talk.

Let's try that, my friends. Because the real blockbuster India needs isn't just expressways and airports—it's civic sense.

CHAPTER 59

FROM JANMABHOOMI TO KARMABHOOMI

Landing in Houston was on time—August 22nd, around 3:50 PM. Yes, I arrived on the same day. That's the beauty of traveling west—you gain time on the clock when flying from India to the USA.

I joined the immigration queue. It was long, as expected. Houston is a major port of entry, and this was peak time for international flights. After waiting for more than 45 minutes, my turn came. Immigration was quick and easy. With the entry stamp on my passport, I headed to the luggage carousel.

I picked up my bags, loaded them on a cart, and pulled out my phone. To my surprise, the phone was dead. I had forgotten to switch it off during the flight. Now I was stranded. My plan was to pick up a rental car from the airport, drive to Sugar Land which was an hour drive, stay overnight at my friend Sudhir Bhai's place, and head to San Antonio the next morning. I had brought some stuff for Bhabhi from India so wanted to hand it over too.

With my phone completely drained, I had no way to inform anyone—not even Rupa—that I had landed safely. Borrowing a stranger's phone wasn't an option here. This isn't India, where during this trip I once faced a similar situation and ended up asking a coconut vendor for his phone. He handed it over with a smile and probably thought, *"This guy wants a call, not a coconut!"*

That trick wouldn't fly in Houston. People here guard their phones like they're holding nuclear codes—and privacy is practically a religion. The reset button was officially pressed. I was in the USA now, and my only lifeline was to hunt down a charging point and bring my phone back to life—like reviving a patient in the ER.

I asked a security person where I could find the nearest charging point. I was almost at the exit gate when he pointed me to a seating area with charging ports. I heaved a sigh of relief. Maneuvering the cart wasn't easy, and I had little energy left. Jet lag was kicking in, and I still had an hour's drive ahead.

I parked the cart and plugged in my phone. After a few minutes, the AT&T logo appeared with its familiar tune. I gave it a few more minutes to come alive properly. The very first thing I did was call Rupa.

She said, "We've been trying to call you for the last hour! We were tracking your flight and getting worried."

I explained the dead phone saga. She said, "Welcome! And guess what? There's a surprise waiting for you."

Turns out, my neighbor Uttam from San Antonio was in Houston for an official assignment and planned to leave that evening. Perfect! No solo drive in jet lag. Just sit and relax in the front seat. I canceled my rental car booking—it was from Costco, so no advance paid. All good.

I called Uttam to check when he could make it to the airport. He said he was still wrapping up work and planned to start in half an hour. His location? Richmond area—almost an hour from the airport. So, I had to wait at least 90 minutes before he could pick me up.

I did some quick math and called him back. "Rather than me waiting at the airport, I'll book a cab and come to your location. By then, you'll be done, and we can start for San Antonio from there."

He was reluctant—worried about my luggage—but I convinced him.

I asked him to share his exact location and booked an Uber . I pushed my cart outside the terminal, looking for the rideshare waiting area. A man approached me. “Sir, where do you want to go? Need a taxi?” He looked Indian but later I found he was from Pakistan. I said no, as I had already booked a cab. I thought he would leave, but he didn’t.

“Sir, have you booked an Uber XL?”

“No,” I said. Uber XL was pricey. I thought I could manage the luggage in a regular Uber.

He said, “No Sir, you need an Uber XL. If you’re interested, I can take you for the same price.”

He had a point. I agreed. “Okay, let me cancel the Uber ride.” After canceling, I got into his cab—a full-size black sedan, well maintained.

We started talking in Hindi, which broke the ice. I asked him to stop at a gas station as I was super thirsty and wanted a bottle of water. He stopped after a few exits. I finished my quick shopping. He waited in the car. When I came out, I saw a black sedan parked and opened the back door to get in. Wrong car! His car was parked next to it. Both were black sedans. He came out and said, “Sir, here I am.” I quickly apologized to the other guy and hopped into the right car.

On the way, we talked about different topics, including the geopolitical situation of India- Pakistan. Traffic was normal, even though it was Friday evening. Google Maps showed 10 minutes to reach the destination, but I wasn’t seeing any commercial setup—just rows of houses. Where was Uttam’s office?

Turns out, he was meeting his colleague visiting Houston on an official trip from India. I met her too. She was Bengali, and I'm half Bengali, so we discussed common topics. Uttam was dropping her at her ex-boss's house where she was staying.

After 10–15 minutes, Uttam and I started our journey to San Antonio. We traveled west, taking ALT 90, then a bit of 183 before merging onto I-10 at Luling. We had driven this route umpteen times. Conversation flowed. I was mostly vocal in the beginning, sharing the good and bad parts of my India visit—mostly good things about my motherland.

But in between, we took I-10 East instead of I-10 West. We drove 10–15 miles before I noticed the map directing us to make a U-turn. I told Uttam. He didn't pay much attention at first. Soon, we realized something was wrong. He reset the map—same directive: take a U-turn at the next exit. That's when we realized we were driving back to Houston! Thank God to the ever-attentive GPS. Without it, we'd be getting farther from home every minute. Uttam took the next exit, and now we were on I-10 West, heading home. This had never happened to us before on this route.

Rupa and Smita (Uttam's wife) kept calling to check when we'd reach. We didn't tell them about the goof-up. The kids were waiting at home to welcome Daddy and have a late dinner. We stopped for gas and coffee. After that, it was a smooth ride. By midnight, we reached home. The kids were tired and had fallen asleep.

I was craving homemade ginger tea. It was ready. We sipped tea and told them about the interesting goof-up that added to our travel time. Ultimately, yours truly was back home.

From Janmabhoomi to Karmabhoomi. I returned not just to San Antonio, but to myself—with humor in my pocket, hope in my heart and a renewed promise: **to live every day as if it's a fresh landing.**